FALSE

POSITIVE

Elsyprema Rajan

TABLE OF CONTENTS

DEDICATION

First and foremost, I would like to express my deepest gratitude to God, whose wisdom, guidance, and strength have made this journey possible. Without His unwavering presence in my life, this book would not have come to fruition.

I am incredibly grateful to my parents, Rajan and Prema Rajan, whose love, encouragement, and constant belief in me have been the foundation of everything I have achieved. Your sacrifices and support have shaped who I am today, and I dedicate this work to you.

To my dear sisters, Hepsyprema Rajan and Felsyprema Rajan, thank you for your endless love and motivation and for always pushing me to do my best. Your encouragement has kept me going during challenging times, and I could not have asked for better support.

Thanking all friends — your belief in me, your support, and your presence in my life have meant the world.

This book is dedicated to young people—may it inspire, motivate, and guide you as you discover your purpose and path. It is written with the hope that it helps you navigate life's challenges and equips you with the tools to grow and succeed.

I would also like to acknowledge the contributions of all those who have inspired, guided, or challenged me along the way. This book would not be what it is without your influence.

Finally, I would like to express my heartfelt thanks to my readers. Your support and enthusiasm for this work mean more to me than words can express. It is my hope that this book brings value, encouragement, and insight into your life.

With sincere gratitude,

Elsyprema Rajan

ABOUT THE AUTHOR

Elsy Prema is a devoted writer passionate about spreading messages of hope, faith, and purpose. With a PhD in Machine Learning, Sustainability, and AI, Elsy combines her academic expertise with her personal journey of faith and observations from nature to inspire others through her writing.

Motivated by her own challenges and triumphs, Elsy writes with both passion and compassion, seeking to connect deeply with her audience. She is deeply passionate about observing nature and perceiving things from different perspectives. She loves to integrate her observations with the Word of God. Through her work, she aims to bring encouragement, renewal, and a sense of direction to those striving to grow in their faith.

Introduction:

False Positives and Discovering Our True Place in the Universe

In the endless expanse of the universe, the stars, planets, and galaxies spin and spiral, creating a celestial tapestry so grand that it defies comprehension. From the moment of the Big Bang, the cosmos has stretched and evolved, growing into a universe that now spans roughly 93 billion light-years. Against this cosmic backdrop, we are just a tiny presence, a single life among billions, pondering our place within this extraordinary creation. The question we all face, echoing through both time and space, is this: *"Where do I fit in this vast universe?"*

This book is an invitation to journey inward, to explore not just the vastness of the cosmos but the landscapes of the soul. The search for purpose and belonging is deeply personal, and it goes beyond what is visible, leading us to confront the limits of our own perception and understanding. To find our place, we must first look beyond the illusions that can deceive us, inviting us to examine not only the universe around us but the truths within us.

One of the most profound examples of this is found right above us in the night sky. As we look up, the stars appear as tiny points of light, while the sun and the moon stand out as dominant, shining bodies. To our eyes, the stars seem small and distant, easily overshadowed by the larger presence of the sun and moon. But in reality, this perception is an illusion. The stars we see may be far larger than our sun—colossal supergiants like Betelgeuse, which

1

could encompass our solar system, dwarfing the sun in size and brilliance. And yet, because of their incredible distance from Earth, they appear to us as pinpricks of light, small and almost insignificant.

To put this in perspective, consider some of these extraordinary stars scattered across our galaxy. **Betelgeuse**, a red supergiant in the constellation Orion, is one of the brightest stars visible in the Northern Hemisphere's winter sky. Its size and brightness eclipse that of our sun by orders of magnitude. **Antares**, another red supergiant residing in the constellation Scorpius and visible during summer months, further exemplifies this magnitude. Stars even more massive, like **VY Canis Majoris**, a red hypergiant approximately 1,500 times larger in diameter than our sun, or **UY Scuti** and **WOH G64**, stand as incomprehensible giants. Located in the constellation Scutum and the Large Magellanic Cloud, respectively, these stars measure up to nearly 2,000 times the size of our sun.

Here, our eyes become instruments of false positives. The stars, when seen from Earth, seem tiny and unimpressive, yet in reality, they are vast and powerful entities burning across unimaginable distances. Our senses record a "truth" that feels accurate because it aligns with what we see, yet this truth is incomplete, a mere shadow of reality. Just as our eyes store the image of stars as small and unremarkable, our mind and heart can store impressions and beliefs that feel true but do not reflect the deeper, divine reality of who we are and what we are meant to become.

This is the essence of a false positive—a belief or perception that feels right but does not align with the greater truth. It is a concept often used in science and statistics, where data might incorrectly signal a result that isn't actually there. In our personal and spiritual lives, we encounter similar "false positives" when we accept surface impressions or fleeting roles as our true purpose. We might feel that a certain job, relationship, or achievement defines us, only to later realize that it wasn't the path God intended. Like mistaking the stars for small, we can misinterpret our role in the universe, accepting a diminished vision of ourselves.

But why do we so readily accept these illusions? Why does it feel so natural to believe what our senses tell us, even if it may not be the whole truth? Part of this lies in the limitations of our perception. Just as our eyes rely on distance and perspective to form an image, our minds rely on experiences, beliefs, and societal values to shape our understanding of self and purpose. When we rely solely on what feels immediately true, we may end up storing "false data"—experiences or beliefs that feel real but lack the depth of divine truth. This false data can influence how we think, feel, and make choices, leading us away from the calling God has woven into our lives.

Imagine for a moment that your mind is a repository, constantly gathering information from the world around you. Like a computer system, it collects inputs and generates outputs. The inputs are your experiences, beliefs, emotions, and societal influences; the output is the feeling or sense of purpose that you carry. If the input is based on incomplete truths or distorted perceptions, the output will be equally distorted, leading you to feel small, insignificant, or misaligned with your true calling. When we store false positives as truths, we create a version of ourselves that may feel right but is far from the purpose God has intended for us.

The journey of discovering our true place in the universe, then, requires us to move beyond these illusions. Just as scientists develop rigorous methods to distinguish true results from false positives, we, too, must learn to discern what is genuine from what only appears to be. This discernment is not a matter of logic alone; it is a spiritual journey, one that requires prayer, reflection, and a willingness to seek God's guidance above our own limited understanding.

As we step into this journey, I invite you to approach each chapter as part of a path that leads to deeper clarity and alignment with your true purpose. This book is not about finding one ultimate answer but about uncovering layers of understanding, each revealing a more profound sense of meaning. Every chapter will encourage you to look past the false positives that may cloud your perception and challenge you to seek the purpose that God has woven uniquely into your life.

Our exploration will move from the vastness of the universe to the intricacies of our lives, encouraging us to discover the places where we have perhaps accepted illusions as truth. With each step, we'll be invited to recognize the ways that God's vision extends beyond what our eyes can see, offering us a calling that is richer and more fulfilling than any illusion could provide.

In the chapters that follow, we'll begin by observing the natural world, finding symbols and reflections of divine purpose in creation around us. From there, we'll delve into the heart of our experiences and beliefs, questioning the impressions we have stored and uncovering the truths that lie beneath. Together, we'll cultivate a vision that sees beyond immediate appearances, moving toward a life that is not only aligned with truth but also in harmony with God's grand design.

This journey is a call to seek clarity and trust that each of us has a place and a role in a purpose greater than ourselves. As we peel back these layers of false positives and illusions, may we find ourselves stepping closer to the essence of who we are, answering not only the question of where we fit in this vast universe but also discovering the deeper joy of living in alignment with our true purpose.

Let us now begin this journey, embracing each insight, each chapter, as a step toward uncovering the place prepared for us in this extraordinary, divinely crafted universe.

CHAPTER 1:
ECHOES OF PURPOSE

In my search for answers, I began by observing the world around me. One sight that never failed to capture my attention was the coconut tree—a common, unassuming presence in my southern Indian hometown. Though simple in appearance, this tree taught me an important lesson about purpose. The coconut tree, with its resilience and versatility, showed me that everything has a reason for being. In fact, the tree has nine valuable parts, each with its own role, each offering something unique and indispensable to the world around it.

The coconut tree, often overlooked as part of the landscape, is a marvel of resourcefulness. The fibrous **husk** of the coconut, for instance, serves as more than just a tough outer shell. Locals often weave it into durable mattresses or use it as kindling for fires. Its fibers are twisted into ropes or crafted into intricate toys that entertain children and adults alike. The **shell**, tough and resilient, is repurposed as an eco-friendly alternative to charcoal, and skilled artisans mold it into beautiful handicrafts. The **flesh** of the coconut, known for its richness and nutrition, is enjoyed raw, cooked, or processed, forming a staple in many dishes. Meanwhile, the **water** inside is revered not just as a refreshing drink but as a nutrient-rich elixir that revitalizes the body and even helps heal ailments.

The **leaves** of the coconut tree are equally versatile, transformed into hats, baskets, and mats, while the sturdy **midribs** are crafted into brooms or skewers. Beneath the leaves lies the **heart of the palm**, or *palmis*, a rare delicacy cherished for its unique flavor. Even the protective **spathe** and **inflorescence**—the flowering part of the tree—are utilized and fashioned into polished containers or other practical items. The **trunk** once provided structural support for homes, while the **roots**, firmly anchored in the earth, are known for their medicinal qualities and valued for treating various ailments. Every part of the coconut tree serves a purpose, embodying a remarkable spirit of resourcefulness that sustains the lives of those around it.

The lessons from the coconut tree reminded me of something similar in a different setting: a community garden. In a nearby town, I once saw a community come together to transform an empty plot into a thriving garden. Each plant was carefully chosen—not one was planted without purpose. Some provided fresh produce, others attracted pollinators, and a few were herbs valued for their healing properties. I realized that this garden, like the coconut tree, was a testament to how intentional choices could turn a barren space into a source of nourishment and life. Every small act of planting, tending, and nurturing contributed to something meaningful and lasting.

This realization lingered with me. If the coconut tree and the community garden could serve so many, each part fulfilling its role with purpose, then what about my own life? What seeds was I planting, and what kind of garden was I nurturing within myself? I began to wonder if, like the people tending the garden, we all have the capacity to make small, intentional choices that build toward something greater. This question stirred in me a deeper curiosity— a desire to understand how I could cultivate purpose daily and find my place in the larger design of life.

As I reflected on the holistic utility of the coconut tree, I began to wonder: If every part of this tree has a role, doesn't that imply I am also here for a reason? This realization sparked a journey of introspection—a quest to understand my own purpose. If even a tree, rooted in one place, plays such a significant role in the ecosystem, then what role was I, a human being, meant to fulfill in this world?

This question became a guiding force, pushing me to explore what it means to have clarity of vision and a deeper sense of purpose in life.

The lesson from the coconut tree led me to a more profound observation. If all living things have a role in the larger design of life, then where do I stand in the grand scheme of existence? This raised an intriguing question: if the coconut tree has value and purpose that are made even more meaningful by human presence, could it be that humanity holds a unique significance? While plants and animals serve essential roles in the ecosystem, it's possible that humans hold a distinct place, perhaps even greater in importance, as we were created with the ability to recognize, harness, and celebrate the purpose of all things around us.

This idea led me to consider whether our purpose is intricately linked not only to our surroundings but also to the very sequence of creation itself.

Reflecting on the order of creation offers another perspective. Why weren't humans created on the first day? This sequence of creation, as outlined in the Bible, can be seen as an expression of God's care and intention. Everything was meticulously prepared— each day brought a new layer of the world into being, setting the stage for the arrival of humankind. Doesn't this sequence reveal the reverence and intrinsic worth that God has woven into each of us? Our very existence feels like a privilege, a testament to the value placed upon us in the divine order.

Understanding this value changes our perspective. It brings a new dimension to our search for purpose, helping us realize that each of us is part of a larger, intentional design. But this knowledge sparks an even deeper question: Beyond the collective purpose shared by humanity, what unique role do I, as an individual, play within this grand universe?

In my own journey, this question grew louder during a solo trip through the Western Ghats. Surrounded by the serenity of nature, I felt connected to something far greater than myself. Each night, as I gazed up at the starlit sky, I was struck by the vastness of the universe and yet felt profoundly connected to it all. This feeling both comforted and unsettled me, revealing my smallness while hinting at a sense of belonging.

One evening, by a campfire, an elderly local approached and began to share his wisdom. Our conversation turned to the mysteries of life, the universe, and purpose. He shared ancient stories of people who had also wrestled with the same questions I faced—stories passed down through generations. One tale, in particular, remains vivid in my memory. It was about a young woman named Lavenya.

Lavenya grew up in a nearby village and felt a profound sense of discontent with the routines of village life. The death of her father left her feeling hollow, questioning her existence and purpose. Determined to find answers, she decided to venture to the highest peak in the Ghats, where, according to local legend, a sacred banyan tree awaited. Beneath this tree, it was said, many seekers had found clarity and purpose. With her father's old diary as a guide, she set out on her journey.

The ascent was arduous. Each step challenged not only her physical strength but also her resolve. Finally, after days of trekking, she reached the summit, expecting to find the legendary tree. Instead, she encountered an elderly woman quietly sipping tea and gazing at the horizon. Disappointed, Lavenya shared her quest with the woman, who listened with patience and understanding. After a thoughtful silence, the woman handed her a simple mirror.

"Look into this and tell me what you see," she instructed. Lavenya, hoping for a revelation, looked into the mirror, but all she saw was her own weary reflection. The woman then told her, "What

9

you seek is not out here but within you. You carry your father's legacy and God's love within you. Your purpose is not a mystery to be solved; it is a story you write every day with your choices. You weren't born coincidentally—you were born with great purpose."

Overwhelmed, Lavenya's heart swelled with understanding. As she opened her father's diary, she found an entry that echoed the woman's wisdom: "Your purpose is illuminated in God's Word. Seek it, live it, and reflect His love." Her journey had shown her that purpose was not something to discover externally but something to cultivate and live out daily.

Inspired by Lavenya's story, I began to consider the true meaning of vision and purpose. Are these simply goals to reach, or is there something deeper at play? It's easy to let words like purpose, aim, goal, and vision blend together, but understanding their distinct meanings helps us grasp their unique roles in our lives.

Imagine purpose as the roots of a tree, hidden from view yet essential for growth, nourishment, and stability. Purpose is what anchors us, grounding our lives with meaning. The trunk represents vision, connecting the roots with the branches above, guiding us upward as we grow. Vision holds our purpose and translates it into direction, pushing us toward our aspirations.

The branches symbolize our aims, extending outward in various directions. Like branches that adapt and change, our aims may shift as circumstances evolve, providing us with diverse experiences along the way. Finally, the leaves represent our goals—specific, measurable achievements that give visible evidence of our growth and progress. Like leaves capturing sunlight to nourish the tree, our goals are the tangible manifestations of our aspirations, reflecting how far we've come.

This metaphor of a tree illustrates the interdependence of purpose, vision, aims, and goals. Purpose nourishes, vision directs, aims expand, and goals fulfill. Together, they form a cohesive whole, supporting and reflecting each other. But as we delve into this journey, one question remains: Where does purpose come from? How do we find the roots of our existence, and what sustains our vision?

This book invites you to explore these questions and discover where you truly belong, peeling back the layers of perception to find the clarity and alignment that reveal your unique place in this world.

CHAPTER 2:

OBSERVING GOD'S VISION THROUGH THE SOUNDS OF THE UNIVERSE

In this chapter, we will journey through the sounds of the universe, from the sun to the stars, the moon, and the planets, as we explore how each celestial body worships God and fulfills its purpose. These heavenly bodies, though without choice or consciousness as we understand it, know their place in creation, each one carrying out its duty with unwavering faithfulness. Through their unique sounds—vibrations that echo across space—they testify to God's majesty, obedience, and order. Even without a will of their own, they serve as powerful examples of loyalty to God's design.

As we observe these cosmic elements, we'll discover how their steadfast obedience, silent yet profound, calls us to consider our own purpose. If the stars, planets, and galaxies—lifeless as we know them—can proclaim God's glory, how much more can we, who are gifted with free will and understanding, find our purpose within His grand design?

Imagine standing alone in the stillness of the night, with the vastness of the universe stretching before you. As you look up at the stars, each brilliant point of light pulses with life, whispering stories as old as time. It's easy to think of space as silent, but science and faith alike reveal that the universe is alive with sound—a breathtaking, celestial symphony that God Himself conducts.

The **sun**, our life-giving star, is a cosmic drummer. Nearly 93 million miles away, it emits vibrations that ripple across its surface like an unceasing heartbeat. Though silent to our ears, these waves create a deep, steady pulse. Imagine it: a drumbeat that has sustained life for billions of years. This rhythm embodies God's faithfulness, like a heartbeat that pulses with warmth and energy, creating an ordered rhythm in the vast expanse of space. **Each morning, when the sun rises, it's as if God's hand lifts the drumstick again, reminding us that He is constant, filling the universe with light, warmth, and life. Just as the sun's rhythm sustains physical life, so does God's love sustain us spiritually.**

Now, consider the **moon**. Though it emits no sound, its influence on Earth is profound. The moon's gravitational pull orchestrates the tides, creating a rhythm that can be felt on every shore. Imagine the ocean's waves rising and falling like a gentle, timeless breath—a silent melody as natural as inhaling and exhaling. If we could hear the moon's "song," perhaps it would be a soft, steady drumbeat—a subtle background to the grander music. Through the moon, God's presence shows us that He moves us in quiet ways, guiding us by rhythms invisible to the eye yet unmistakable in effect. **The moon's silent command over the tides is like God's gentle guidance in our lives. Just as the ocean rises and falls in harmony with the moon, we are called to align our lives with God's unseen hand, trusting in His quiet but powerful influence.**

Above us, the **stars** add their voices to this symphony. Each star vibrates at a unique frequency, producing waves that vary in pitch and tone. Younger stars hum with bright, energetic notes, while older stars resonate with deep, ancient tones. Imagine standing under the night sky and hearing each star's melody as it radiates across light-years, filling the cosmos with a chorus that is both ancient and fresh, vast and intimate. This celestial choir, this hymn of praise, spans the universe, echoing the glory of a Creator who takes joy in the beauty and variety of His work. **Even as stars age** and change, their frequencies shift and evolve, yet their place in the heavens remains. **This is a reminder that, like the stars, we may change through the seasons of our lives, but our purpose and calling in God's creation endure.**

Then, there are the **planets**, each with its own unique "voice." Jupiter, the solar system's giant, produces a low, rumbling sound like distant thunder, while Saturn hums with an ethereal, bell-like resonance. These planetary sounds, captured by scientists as low-frequency waves, contribute depth and mystery to the universe. Picture each planet as a unique instrument in God's orchestra: Jupiter, a grand bass; Saturn, a haunting bell; Earth—a quiet, melodic hum—contributing to a soundscape that is not chaotic but perfectly composed. **Each planet's orbit and sound are woven into God's perfect order, reminding us that, even when our lives feel chaotic, there is an unseen rhythm and purpose orchestrated by God's hand.** Each planet moves according to God's design, reflecting His creativity and order in ways that defy human comprehension.

On **Earth**, the symphony continues with the vibrant sounds of life. The wind rustling through leaves, rivers flowing over stones, birds singing at dawn—all these sounds unite in a song of creation. Imagine that each morning, as the sun rises, Earth's creatures join in a natural chorus, celebrating the life they have been given. The rustling trees, the crashing waves, the quiet forests—they are like verses in a song that praise the Creator. **Earth, as a unique planet teeming with life, adds a living layer to this divine harmony. Every living being—each tree, river, and bird—testifies to God's presence in creation, inviting us to pause and listen to the beauty of God's handiwork all around us.** The oceans roar with strength while the mountains stand in silent reverence. Even deserts, with their quiet stillness, offer a peaceful, unspoken worship.

What's more, each of us is part of this symphony. Our hearts beat in rhythm, our breaths add a soft cadence, and our lives contribute notes to God's melody. When we show love, offer kindness, seek truth, or pursue purpose, we add our voices to a timeless song. Our thoughts, choices, and actions become instruments of praise, unique melodies that blend into the grand music of creation. **We are the only creatures with the conscious ability to join this worship knowingly, to decide each day to align our lives with God's purpose. This unique capacity to choose is a gift, a reminder that we have a place not only in the physical creation but in God's heart.** We're not just audience members; we're part of the orchestra, created to harmonize with the sounds of the universe in a way that reflects God's vision and love.

This cosmic symphony stirs our souls, calling us to consider our place in the vastness. Each element fulfills a purpose, each sound expresses meaning, and each moment in creation resonates with God's presence. The sun beats with power, the moon moves with grace, the stars sing with radiance, and the Earth echoes with life. Through this symphony, God reveals Himself, inviting us to listen, to marvel, and to praise. As we hear the universe's song, we catch a glimpse of eternity—a beauty so profound it leaves us humbled, a call so powerful it stirs us to join in.

As we listen, we are reminded of our own calling to worship. Just as each star has a unique tone, each planet has its own hum, and every creature has its distinct song, we, too, are called to live in harmony with God's love, wisdom, and grace. This is the universe's song—a song of creation, purpose, and worship. **Psalm 19:1 reminds us, "The heavens declare the glory of God; the skies proclaim the work of His hands." As part of creation, we join this testimony, letting our lives reflect the beauty and intention that God has woven into the fabric of the universe.** We are invited to join in, adding our voices to the symphony that fills the heavens.

In the vastness of the universe, God's love for us resonates as He invites us to find our place in this divine melody, to live lives that echo His beauty, and to let our own notes play in harmony with the music of eternity.

But here's something to ponder: these cosmic wonders—the sun, moon, stars, and planets—are lifeless as we understand life, yet they still "sing." Though they cannot think, feel, or make choices, they fulfill their roles in the grand design with a kind of silent loyalty. Day after day, they move in their orbits, shine with their light, and influence Earth in ways that sustain life, obeying God's natural laws with unswerving faithfulness. **How often do we, as humans with free will and understanding, resist our own calling? Nature and the cosmos fulfill their purpose without question. Are we willing to do the same?**

Their unwavering obedience and their silent praise speak of a cosmic humility, a devotion without question or doubt. They don't grow weary or seek to change their roles. Without a will of their own, they declare God's glory with simple, steadfast presence, each one a testament to order, purpose, and awe. They do what they were created to do, producing their sounds and their rhythms in perfect harmony.

So here's a question for us: if the sun and stars, the planets and moons—creations without thought or choice—live so perfectly in harmony with God's vision, what does that mean for us? We have been given life, thought, and the freedom to choose. We can sing, speak, and create in ways no star or planet ever could. Yet, do we always live with the same sense of purpose? **As we watch the stars in their silent obedience, we're called to reflect on our own lives: Are we embracing our God-given roles, allowing our actions to resonate in harmony with His design, or are we creating discord by seeking our own way?**

Unlike the stars, we have a song that is ours alone. Each of us has a voice, a unique rhythm, and the ability to choose how we will play our part in this divine orchestra. But with this freedom comes a deeper calling: to seek our true place, to listen for God's rhythm, and to let our lives resonate in harmony with His vision. It's as if God has given each of us a melody, and we are invited to add our notes to the symphony to weave our lives into a greater story, one that has been playing long before us and will continue long after.

So, as we look up to the stars and witness their silent obedience, perhaps we are invited to ask ourselves: How will we add our voices? Will we, like the sun, shine with a purpose that fuels life around us? Will we, like the moon, bring a quiet, steady influence that others can lean on? Will we, like the stars, find our unique place in the heavens and sing our song in harmony with the universe?

The stars and planets sing with simplicity and certainty. But we are gifted with something more—a life filled with potential, a heart capable of love, and a soul that can worship with wonder. The choice is ours. Will we, too, join in this song of creation, allowing our lives to be a melody that rises with the sun and rests with the stars? Will we become part of the symphony that fills the universe with praise?

As we ponder this, may we find our own notes to add, letting our lives sing in harmony with God's masterpiece, a worship that is both unique and eternal.

CHAPTER 3:

FINDING OUR PLACE THROUGH GOD'S CREATION

In the chapters ahead, we'll delve into the lives of some of God's most unique creations, observing how they each find their place in the world with a purpose so natural, so aligned, that they seem to know exactly why they were created. As we explore these lives, we'll uncover a hidden wisdom—a guiding assurance that, though they are not human, these creatures embody qualities that call us to reflect on our own lives.

What can we learn from an eagle's clarity, an ant's dedication, a plant's silent growth, or a spider's creative persistence? Each creature brings a quiet lesson: they live with a natural trust in God's provision and faithfulness to the role they've been given, never questioning their place but rather embracing it fully. They show us that living with purpose and hope isn't just about understanding; it's about faithfully walking the path set before us with an inner knowing that we belong.

In the chapters that follow, we'll look closely at these unique lives. Through them, we'll find inspiration to discover our own place, to live with the same unshakeable hope and gratitude, knowing that, like them, we are part of something greater. We, too, have a role to play in God's intricate design, and in finding it, we fulfill a calling far beyond ourselves.

The Eagle's Silent Sermon

As I sat beneath the vast, open sky, a question stirred in my soul: Where do I fit in this universe that God has created? It's a question that weighs on the heart, one that asks us to look deeper than the life we live day by day. In moments like this, I often look to God's creation for answers. In one of His most majestic creatures, the eagle, I found some powerful lessons that not only illuminate our earthly journey but also reflect the life we are called to live in Christ.

The Bible often uses the eagle as a symbol of strength, renewal, and God's faithful provision. Isaiah 40:31 tells us, "But those who hope in the Lord will renew their strength. They will soar on wings like eagles; they will run and not grow weary; they will walk and not faint." The eagle's life, when viewed through the lens of Scripture, offers us profound lessons about who we are in Christ and how we are meant to live out our purpose in God's grand design.

The sun was just beginning to sink behind the hills when I found myself by the cliff's edge, watching as the wind danced through the tall grass. The air was crisp, with the faint sound of a distant river echoing through the valley. Above me, a lone eagle traced circles in the sky—its wings cutting through the heavens in effortless grace. I stood, captivated, as if the eagle was preaching a silent sermon, one written not with words but with the essence of its being.

Something stirred in me as I watched, a question that had often whispered itself into my thoughts: Where do I fit in this vast universe? It's a question that presses on the heart of every soul, especially in the quiet moments when life itself seems to pause. In that stillness, I realized that perhaps the answer wasn't just in the asking but in the observing. God's creation speaks if we have ears to listen. And on that evening, the eagle began to reveal its secrets.

The eagle's journey begins with its sheer size, an undeniable reflection of power and presence. With wings that span over seven feet, the eagle doesn't just inhabit the sky—it owns it. It soars with an understanding that it belongs up there, that it was made to rise above. And yet, it does not rise by its own strength alone. The wind, invisible yet constant, carries it higher.

Is this not the story of faith? We, too, were made to soar, not by our own strength, but by the power of Christ. It's easy to feel small in this world, to wonder if our lives hold any true significance. But when we trust in Jesus, we begin to see the grandeur of God's plan. Like the eagle, we are meant to rise above the noise, above the distractions, and fly with purpose. His grace spreads our wings, and we are carried by the wind of His Spirit. When we truly trust, we begin to live boldly, knowing we were created for more than the mundane—we were created to soar.

And then there's the vision—that piercing gaze that can spot prey from miles away. The eagle's eyes are sharper than we can imagine, focused and unwavering. It sees what is often hidden, honing in on its goal with precision. It reminds me of Jesus' call for us to fix our eyes on Him, the One who goes before us, the One who sees beyond the immediate and calls us to a life of eternal purpose.

How often are we blinded by the world? Distracted by fleeting pleasures and empty pursuits? Jesus doesn't ask us to see with earthly eyes. No—He calls us to see through the lens of faith, to have spiritual vision. Like the eagle, we are called to see beyond the surface, to look past the temporary and into the eternal. When our eyes are fixed on Christ, we see differently. We see the purpose in pain, the beauty in brokenness, and the strength that comes from surrender.

As I watched the eagle descend with purpose, talons outstretched, I thought of faith. Those talons, sharp and strong, are meant to grasp and hold on. They are relentless, designed to secure what is needed for survival. How much more are we called to cling to the promises of God with a faith that does not waver? When the storms of life come—and they will—our grip on Jesus is what keeps

20

us grounded. His Word is our lifeline, a foundation that does not crumble under pressure.

Just as the eagle grasps with precision, we must hold tightly to the truths of Christ. Faith is not a passive belief; it's a fierce and unwavering grip on the God who holds all things together. We may not always understand His ways, but we trust that He is faithful. In the midst of doubt, in the face of fear, we do not let go. We cling to the cross, knowing that it is there where true life is found.

There is also beauty in the eagle's design. Its wings are shaped for flight, every feather crafted to capture the wind, and every part of its form fitted for the sky. Each feather, carefully designed, carries the strength and spirit of the creature. How much more, then, are we, as believers, made for God's purposes? Each one of us, with our unique attributes and gifts, is designed with intention. We are not afterthoughts but carefully crafted parts of God's divine plan, each of us made to soar in our own way.

And as the light of the setting sun caught the eagle's plumage, I was struck by its beauty. Each feather was unique, yet together, they formed a magnificent whole. Some eagles, like the Bald Eagle, boast white heads and dark bodies, while others, like the Golden Eagle, shimmer in shades of brown and gold. Every feather has a purpose, and every detail is crafted with care.

This, too, is our story. Psalm 139:14 tells us that we are "fearfully and wonderfully made." Each of us is crafted by the Creator's hand, unique and beautiful in His sight. Like the eagle's plumage, we are not meant to blend in but to reflect His glory in the way we live. Our identity in Christ is not a mask we wear but the very essence of who we are. We are His, created to reveal His love and grace to a world that desperately needs it.

But there's more. The eagle is not just a symbol of power and beauty; it's a symbol of purposeful living. The eagle hunts with precision, taking only what it needs, never wasting the gifts that God provides. In a world obsessed with accumulation and excess, the eagle reminds us of Jesus' words: "Do not worry about your life, what you will eat or drink; or about your body, what you will wear" (Matthew 6:25). Just as the eagle trusts the provision of the Creator, so must we. We are called to live with intention—to trust that God will provide for our needs as we seek first His kingdom.

And then there is the flight—the thing that takes our breath away. The eagle soars, not with frantic flapping, but with calm confidence, riding the currents of the wind. It's in the soaring that we see the ultimate picture of freedom. This is what Christ offers us—freedom from sin, freedom from fear, freedom from the burdens that weigh us down. When we surrender to Him, we rise, carried by His grace.

Yet, even in the freedom of flight, the eagle is not without responsibility. It is fiercely territorial and protective of its nest and the life it builds. Its eyrie, often perched high on unreachable cliffs, is a fortress of safety. This reminds me of Jesus' teaching about building our lives on the solid rock of His Word. When the storms come—and they always will—our foundation must be firm. Like the eagle's nest, our lives are not meant to be fragile. They are meant to stand strong in Christ.

As the eagle circled back to its nest, I thought about the way it returned year after year to the same place, building and rebuilding with faithfulness. Eagles mate for life, committed to the work of creating and protecting their family. This is a picture of God's faithfulness to us. He never leaves us and never gives up on us. Even when we falter, even when we wander, He calls us back to Himself, offering grace upon grace. His love is steadfast, unchanging, eternal. And in Him, we are called to love with that same faithfulness.

The eagle's resilience through time speaks volumes of the patience we are to carry in our lives. Through decades of life, the eagle endures seasons of plenty and of trial, storms and clear skies alike. We are called to this same resilience, to stand through trials and seasons of waiting with hope in God's promises, knowing that He brings us through to places of purpose.

Time passes for the eagle, as it does for us all. The eagle, with its resilience and strength, may live for decades, enduring through seasons and storms. Its life is a testimony to the power of perseverance—a trait Jesus calls us to embrace. "Blessed is the one who perseveres under trial," says James 1:12, "because having stood the test, that person will receive the crown of life that the Lord has promised to those who love Him."

As I stood by that cliff, watching the eagle disappear into the twilight, I felt a deep sense of peace. In its flight, its strength, and its purpose, the eagle seemed to reflect the intricate design of the One who created it. Each movement was purposeful; every beat of its wings seemed to declare that it was living fully in the place it was meant to be. And a question rose in my heart: does the eagle ever question where it belongs or the heights it's meant to reach? It soars as if it knows, without a doubt, that it was made for this—to rise, to claim the sky, to fulfill its calling.

In that moment, the question turned inward: Am I living fully in the place and purpose God has designed for me? Do I see myself as He sees me—capable of soaring by His grace, grounded by His truth, and created for a life beyond the ordinary? The eagle's silent sermon was clear: it lives as a creature confident in its design, trusting fully in the Creator's plan, embracing the skies it was crafted to command. How often do I hold back, uncertain of my worth or afraid of my calling, forgetting that I, too, was crafted with purpose and intentionality?

Where do I fit in this vast universe? Like the eagle, I am called to soar—not by my own power, but by the strength of the One who made me. In Christ, I am not lost in the vastness. I am found, known, and placed. And just as the eagle soars with confidence in the wind that sustains it, so I, too, can rise—renewed, free, and secure in the currents of His grace. In the presence of the One who created the heavens and earth, I can rest assured that I am where I am meant to be, ready to live out the purpose He has woven into my being.

CHAPTER 4:

DILIGENCE IN EVERY STEP

In this chapter, I'm drawn to a tiny yet profound teacher—the ant. With its quiet diligence and steadfast focus, the ant offers us unexpected lessons about purpose and persistence. At first glance, an ant might seem insignificant in the vastness of God's creation, easily overlooked and often unnoticed. Yet, by observing its unwavering work and commitment, we begin to see glimpses of God's wisdom and design. In these small creatures, God has placed a remarkable strength, focus, and determination that can inspire us as we seek to understand our own place and purpose in this life.

One warm summer afternoon, I found myself sitting quietly by the edge of a peaceful lake, lost in thought, when I noticed a line of ants busily at work, gathering food. Their movements were deliberate and orderly, each ant following the one in front of it, all of them collectively following their leader. Watching them, I was struck by their unity and focus, a small community working together to fulfill their purpose.

Out of curiosity, I gently nudged one of the ants from the line, causing it to stray. Immediately, this ant became disoriented, as though lost in a world it no longer recognized. It began to frantically search for its place, scurrying in different directions, trying to find its way back. The line was long, and the ant struggled to rejoin it.

At the same moment, I noticed the ant just behind the one I had disturbed. It didn't seem to care about its fallen companion, nor did it pause to help. It simply followed the leader without question, unaffected by the chaos of the ant that had strayed.

The Unquestioning Follower

This simple observation left a deep impression on me. I realized something profound: in life, it's easy to follow those in front of us, to walk in the footsteps of others without questioning where they are going. But this moment was a clear lesson—do not simply follow the one ahead. Instead, follow the true Leader, Jesus, whose guidance never falters, even when the road before us does. It's a reminder that we, like the ants, must choose our path carefully and seek out the true Leader, lest we find ourselves lost and without purpose.

The Wandering Ant's New Purpose

Returning my attention to the ant I had disturbed, I watched as it continued to search for direction. After wandering for a while, it stumbled upon a small piece of food and became distracted, seemingly abandoning its original mission. This shift made me wonder: had the ant lost its purpose? Was it now wandering aimlessly with no clear goal? At first, I believed it had, thinking, "It's no longer on the path to where it was meant to be." But as I continued watching, another thought emerged: maybe this ant, though diverted, had a unique purpose all along, one that wasn't bound by the same path as the others. Perhaps it was meant to discover something different, to fulfill a calling that only it could achieve.

The more I observed, the more I realized that this small, seemingly insignificant creature held a much deeper lesson. The ant, though wandering alone, carried a small piece of food with it. It was anxious, moving in circles, revisiting the same spots as if searching for answers, unsure of where to go next. In front of it lay the vast expanse of the lake—a barrier it could never cross. The ant seemed trapped, isolated from its companions and unable to move forward.

Yet, something unexpected happened. After pausing for what seemed like an eternity, the ant suddenly changed direction, heading westward toward the place where I sat. Curious, I followed from a distance, careful not to disturb it again. Soon, the ant came upon a group of much larger ants fighting over a small piece of food. Without hesitation, the smaller ant walked right between them. Though I couldn't understand the interaction, it seemed as if the ants communicated, and to my surprise, the larger ants began to follow the smaller ones. The ant, once lost, now led others back to the food it had discovered earlier.

At that moment, a profound realization washed over me. You may feel small in this vast universe, weak and inadequate, especially when your journey seems long and uncertain. You may even feel like you've strayed too far from the path as if you've lost sight of your purpose. But I want to remind you—God has set you apart for a reason. He has a unique calling for you, even if you cannot see it yet. Like the disturbed ant, you are not forgotten. You are not lost. You have been chosen for a distinct purpose that only you can fulfill.

The Hidden Strength of Small Steps

The ants that stayed on their path were diligent, yes, but the real lesson for me came from the ant that strayed. Even in its confusion, it took a small step in a new direction. And that small decision, seemingly insignificant at the time, changed the course of its journey. Sometimes, in our lives, we feel overwhelmed, lost in a sea of obstacles, crying out in the quiet moments, searching for answers in the silence of our struggles. We feel like we cannot move forward because a lake, a mountain, or some other insurmountable barrier stands in our way.

Consider the ants for a moment—when we look at their lives, they seem filled with uncertainty. They have no way of knowing when their time will come or what dangers lie ahead. Yet, despite

27

this uncertainty, they remain committed to their purpose. They work diligently, pursuing their vision and continuously searching for their place of value without ever losing focus on the task at hand.

But, my dear friends, I urge you to remember the story of Joseph. God gave Joseph a vision when he was only 18 years old, but it took more than 12 years for that vision to come to pass. Along the way, Joseph faced trials and hardships that could have easily made him forget the promise God had given him. But the One who placed that vision in his heart never forgot him. And just as God fulfilled His promise to Joseph, He will fulfill His promises to you.

Even if your journey feels long and your vision seems distant, trust in the One who gave it to you. You may not understand the path you're on, but rest assured—God knows exactly where you're meant to be. Every small step you take, no matter how uncertain, is part of His greater plan for your life.

By focusing on the ant's journey from confusion to leadership, we see that our place is found not by fitting into pre-established roles but by recognizing that God has a unique purpose for each of us. Even when we feel out of place or insignificant, we are exactly where we need to be to fulfill that purpose.

As I sat by the lake, watching the ant persist despite its struggles, I found a quiet answer to my own question. Where do I fit in this vast universe? Like the ant, you may feel small, lost, or uncertain at times, but **your place is not defined by your size, strength, or ability. It is defined by the One who guides you. In Christ, even when the path is unclear, you are not forgotten.** With every step, however small, you are moving toward a purpose that He has set for you. And as long as your faith remains in Him, you will find your way—steadfast, resilient, and secure in the place He has prepared for you.

CHAPTER 5:

WEAVING YOUR PLACE IN THE GRAND DESIGN

In this chapter, we're exploring how creation itself mirrors God's design, focusing on the symbolic artistry of the spider's web. The intricate threads it spins reveal lessons on purpose, resilience, and intentionality in ways we may not have considered. Observing a spider carefully weaving its web—choosing its place, laying each strand with precision, and fortifying it against winds—offers us profound insights. These small creatures have no choice in their work; their instincts are divinely designed, guiding them to fulfill their purpose in this vast world. In the same way, we, too, are called to craft a meaningful life woven from experiences, struggles, joys, and challenges that reflect God's masterful design.

One morning during a trip to India, I sat quietly in the garden, captivated by a spider weaving its web near a mango tree. Every movement was filled with purpose; each strand, laid with delicate precision, revealed a silent resolve. The entire process, completed in under an hour, seemed almost sacred. Although the spider's threads were fine and delicate, the web it formed was resilient enough to withstand the elements. As I observed this miniature architect, I began to reflect on how similar we are, each of us weaving the threads of our life story, even when the path seems fragile or the future uncertain.

The Fragility and Strength of Purpose

What struck me most was how the spider kept weaving, undeterred by the delicate nature of its work. Each thread, no matter how thin, had a purpose. And just like that web, our lives are both fragile and strong. Often, it's easy to see our lives as vulnerable and disrupted by the smallest setbacks, yet in God's design, we are given the strength to endure and thrive. In those moments of fragility, we learn the true resilience and purpose of our journey.

Consider this: Are we willing to keep building even when things feel uncertain? Do we recognize that our experiences, both painful and joyful, are threads that God is weaving together? *Psalm 139:14* tells us, "I praise you because I am fearfully and wonderfully made." Each thread of our lives is woven with intention, even when we don't yet understand the full picture.

The Process of Rebuilding

On another day, I observed a different spider that had built its web in the corner of our home. Unaware of the effort involved, my mother quickly swept it away, seeing it as little more than an eyesore. To her, it was something small and dispensable. The spider, sensing danger, quickly scurried away to safety, its home destroyed. I couldn't help but feel sympathy, imagining how many times the spider must start over, undeterred by setbacks.

This moment led me to reflect: How often are we forced to rebuild in life? Sometimes, the things we pour our hearts into may be swept away unexpectedly. But like the spider, we're called to keep creating, even when what we've built is lost. **God calls us to perseverance**—an unshakable resolve that, no matter what, we will not give up on the life and purpose He has called us to fulfill. **Galatians 6:9** reminds us, "Let us not become weary in doing good, for at the proper time we will reap a harvest if we do not give up."

Layers of Meaning in the Spider's Web

The more I observed, the more I noticed how purposeful each thread was. The spider doesn't randomly lay silk; it uses different types of threads, each with a specific purpose:

- **Dragline Silk**: This forms the outer framework and is a lifeline, allowing the spider to escape if needed. In our lives, we also need an anchor—a core belief, a "lifeline" to hold us steady. What is our dragline silk? Is it our faith, our values, or the relationships that ground us? *Psalm 18:2* says, "The Lord is my rock, my fortress, and my deliverer." Like a dragline, God is our foundation.

- **Sticky Spiral Silk**: This is the thread that catches prey, ensuring the spider's sustenance. Just as this thread provides for the spider's needs, we, too, must work toward what sustains us spiritually and physically. Are we "catching" the right things in our lives—truth, growth, and purpose? Are we spending time and effort on what truly nourishes our spirit? *Matthew 6:33* tells us, "Seek first His kingdom and His righteousness, and all these things will be given to you as well."

- **Attachment Silk**: This anchors the web securely. Our lives need solid grounding, a connection to people and values that keep us steady through challenges. Are we attached to God's truth, remaining firm in our faith no matter the storm? *Hebrews 6:19* offers assurance: "We have this hope as an anchor for the soul, firm and secure."

Each type of silk represents a purpose, showing that every element of our lives, no matter how small, plays a role. God has given us the ability to craft a meaningful life, using the "silks" of our talents, experiences, and relationships to form a beautiful web of purpose.

Resilience Through Brokenness

One day, as I observed a spider calmly repairing a broken thread in its web, it struck me how often we, too, must mend the broken strands in our lives. The spider doesn't abandon its web at the first sign of trouble; instead, it patiently returns to repair, rebuild, and continue its work. This resilience speaks to us directly. Life won't always go as planned. Brokenness, loss, and hardship will happen, yet these moments don't have to break us. They can be woven back into our story, creating something even more beautiful.

Are we willing to repair the brokenness in our lives, trusting that even our failures and pain have a purpose? *Isaiah 61:3* reminds us that God gives us "beauty for ashes," and like the spider, we can find new purpose in what seems broken.

Reflecting on the Master's Design

Every thread the spider weaves is a testament to its instincts and its unchanging purpose. Similarly, we are a reflection of God's design, woven to mirror His creativity, wisdom, and love. God's Word tells us that we are "God's handiwork, created in Christ Jesus to do good works, which God prepared in advance for us to do" (*Ephesians 2:10*). Our lives are more than the sum of our parts; they are masterpieces in progress, each thread contributing to a greater design that reflects God's glory.

As I watched the spider complete its web, I realized that our lives, like these delicate structures, serve a purpose. Each success, each struggle, and each seemingly insignificant thread forms a story that reflects the patience, creativity, and vision of our Creator.

Embracing Our Place in the Universe

So, where do we fit in this vast universe? Like the spider, we're called to create, to persevere, and to find meaning in our work. Each thread of our lives—every experience, every decision, every moment—is part of something greater. And when we trust in God's vision, we find that even our challenges are part of His masterpiece.

We don't weave aimlessly; rather, God, as Master Weaver, guides each thread, placing it in just the right place, forming something beautiful even from our brokenness. We are part of His intricate design, crafted to reflect His purpose, grace, and love.

So, as we weave our lives, let's consider this: Are we building with resilience, returning to the work even when it's undone? Are we intentional about each thread, knowing that every part of our journey has meaning? Like the spider, let us create a life that reflects the beauty of our Creator's design, resilient and full of purpose, trusting that each strand we weave holds a place in God's grand design.

CHAPTER 6:
SEEDS OF PURPOSE, THREADS OF CREATION

In this chapter, we'll explore the journey of growth and purpose through the metaphor of a seed. Just as each seed carries within it the potential to become something unique and fruitful, so do our lives contain the threads of purpose waiting to be cultivated and nurtured. Through my father's passion for agriculture, I learned that not every seed can grow just anywhere; it requires specific conditions, cultivated soil, and an environment suited to its nature. This concept invites us to consider our own lives and the environments we seek to grow in. **If even a non-living seed needs the right place to begin its journey, what about us—living beings with unique callings?**

Watching my father plant seeds, I began to understand that, like seeds, our growth and purpose are tied to finding the right "soil." Each seed has a unique purpose, a design intended to bloom and bear fruit, but this can only happen when it is in the right conditions. **In the same way, our purpose is interwoven with the places and seasons in which we are planted. Just as a farmer carefully selects where to plant each seed, God, knowing the uncertainty we face, has a place prepared for each of us.**

Reflecting on the planting process, I realized that just as each seed requires care, time, and patience to grow, so too do we need to embrace the seasons of waiting in our lives. There is a beautiful patience in the natural world that mirrors the journey of finding our place and purpose. Some seeds sprout within days, while others take weeks, months, or even years. **Our lives, too, are unique in the** timelines they follow, and like seeds, we need time to establish roots before we can bear fruit.

Searching for the Right Soil

As humans, we often find ourselves in search of the "right soil"—a place where we can plant ourselves and flourish. In the same way that we carefully choose where to plant a seed, God knows the conditions we need to thrive and prepares a place uniquely suited to us. **His Word even tells us that He has prepared a place for us in eternity, but what about our earthly place in this universe? How do we discover where we are meant to be and grow?**

The answer lies in understanding our purpose. Just as a seed's purpose is to grow and bear fruit, our purpose helps us discover our place in the world. Once we find our purpose, we can confidently say, "I have found my place." This doesn't happen overnight; finding our place often takes time, reflection, and a willingness to grow where we are planted, trusting that the Master Gardener knows the ideal conditions for our journey.

Trusting the Process of Growth

The process of finding where we belong and where we will thrive is not always immediate. Just as farmers seek the right soil and environment for their seeds, so must we seek out places and opportunities that align with our unique purpose. **Some seeds need to be sown at a specific season, while others take longer to sprout, even years. Likewise, each of us has a timeline crafted by God, and we are called to trust that growth is happening, even when we cannot see it.**

Much like seeds, we are each unique in the conditions we need to thrive. Some require sunlight, others shade; some need deep soil, while others only rest near the surface. Each of us has our own path, our own set of circumstances, where we can grow and bear fruit. **The seasons of waiting and trusting the process are vital for building resilience and preparing us for the fruitfulness ahead.**

Embracing Hidden Growth

Growth doesn't happen overnight. Seeds remain hidden beneath the soil for a time before the first sprouts emerge. Likewise, in our lives, we may endure seasons where it feels as if no growth is visible, as if nothing is happening. Yet, during these periods, something vital is unfolding beneath the surface. **Are we willing to trust God in the seasons where our growth is unseen? Are we patient enough to wait for the fruit that only time can reveal?**

When the seed does begin to grow, it doesn't instantly bear fruit. There is a process of development and maturing, where roots need to take hold deep within the soil to draw nourishment from the earth. In our lives, this mirrors how we must draw strength from faith, experience, and the lessons learned along the way. **Each season brings something necessary for our growth, even those that are challenging or seemingly barren.**

Resilience in the Face of Setbacks

A seed faces many obstacles—a gust of wind may blow it away, a lack of rain may cause drought, and predators may come to consume it. Yet the seed, though small, is designed with resilience to survive and ultimately thrive, even in harsh conditions. **Our place in this universe may seem elusive at times, but the resilience God has woven into us ensures we can endure setbacks and find where we belong, even in times of struggle.**

Even when things seem to go wrong, there is a divine resilience within us. Each setback we face has the potential to strengthen our roots, deepen our understanding, and refine our purpose. Just as a plant grows stronger after enduring a storm, so do we emerge with greater resilience and determination to fulfill our purpose.

Finding Our Place in God's Design

So, where do we fit in this vast universe? Like the seed, our place is deeply tied to our purpose. The purpose of a seed is to grow, to bloom, and to bear fruit. When we discover the purpose of our lives, we find our place. We are not planted by accident; we are carefully placed by God to thrive in the season and soil He has chosen for us. **And even when our growth seems slow, when we feel as though nothing is happening, we can trust that each moment is part of a greater plan.**

As the seed waits for the right moment to break through the soil and reach toward the sun, so must we trust that God is working within us, preparing us for the season when we will bear fruit. Each of us is like a seed in the Master Gardener's hands, nurtured by His love and wisdom, growing toward a future we can only glimpse. The journey may be long, and the path may be difficult, but with patience and faith, we will find our place in His grand design, just as He intended from the very beginning.

CHAPTER 7:

PATHS OF GRACE: DISCOVERING GOD'S PURPOSE IN NATURE

In this chapter, we'll delve deeply into the purpose of life, exploring how our "place" in the universe is intricately tied to our purpose. When we think about purpose, it's essential to recognize that while everyone's purpose is unique, it's distinct from our personal goals. A goal is something we set for ourselves, but purpose is something that God has woven into us. Our goals are often simple to define, like markers we want to reach, but purpose—the reason we exist, the design God has for us—invites us into something far deeper and more meaningful.

Nature's Reflection of God's Design

Imagine walking through nature—a quiet forest, the babble of a stream, mountains rising in the distance, each element serving a purpose without striving or comparison. Every tree, river, and mountain holds a specific role in God's creation, and none exist without reason. The tree doesn't set a goal to bear fruit; it simply follows its purpose, producing fruit naturally when rooted in good soil and nourished. In the same way, God calls us to grow in alignment with our purpose, trusting in His rhythm and timing rather than rushing the process.

Just as every part of nature serves its purpose, our lives, too, fit into God's grand design. Every part of creation, from the mighty river to the tiniest insect, fulfills a role and thrives in its season. In this, we are reminded that God has also shaped us uniquely, with a purpose that we are called to discover and fulfill.

God's Timing and Seasons

Nature moves in seasons—times of growth, rest, renewal, and harvest. Each phase has value, and none rushes to the next. In our lives, there are seasons where purpose feels vibrant and clear, but there are also winter seasons where it seems dormant, and everything feels still. During these times, it's easy to feel that nothing is happening, but just as nature trusts the seasons, we are called to trust God's timing.

Consider the story of Noah. When God called Noah to build an ark, he obeyed despite the decades it would take and the ridicule he faced from those around him. Noah spent years building the ark, trusting in a purpose he couldn't fully see. There were no signs of rain, no evidence that his task would ever make sense to others. Yet Noah's faith in God's promise sustained him through every long day, every challenge, and every doubt. Through Noah's patience, we see a profound example of waiting on God's timing and the faith required to fulfill our purpose even when the path ahead is unclear. In time, God's plan was revealed, and Noah's obedience preserved life. His story reminds us that waiting on God's timing allows His purpose to unfold in ways beyond our understanding.

Purpose vs. Goal

As we journey through life, it's common to set goals—clear, tangible targets that we aspire to achieve. A goal might be completing a degree, securing a particular job, or achieving personal milestones. Goals give us direction, motivation, and a sense of accomplishment. But while goals are often based on our desires and achievements, purpose is about aligning our lives with God's vision for us.

Purpose is not necessarily about what we accomplish but about who we are becoming in Christ. Unlike goals, which we reach and then move beyond, purpose is enduring and unfolds over time. It's woven into the fabric of our identity and guides us throughout life. Purpose brings depth and meaning to each moment, whereas goals can sometimes leave us feeling empty after the initial satisfaction fades.

Consider again the example of a tree in nature. A tree's "goal," if it were to set one, might be to grow taller or produce more fruit. However, its true purpose is to fulfill the unique role God has assigned it—to offer shade, support life, and create beauty. Even when a tree isn't producing visible fruit, it's still living out its purpose by growing, anchoring the soil, and providing a habitat.

Our goals are temporary, but our purpose is eternal. Goals may shift with life's circumstances, but God's purpose for us remains constant. Pursuing goals in alignment with our purpose brings fulfillment and joy because we are living as God intended. In contrast, achieving goals that are separate from our purpose can feel unfulfilling, as they may not align with our deeper calling.

Walking the Path with Faith

Life is much like a winding path through the unknown. When we walk in nature, we may not see what lies ahead, yet with faith, we trust that the path will lead us where we need to be. Psalm 119:105 reminds us, "Your word is a lamp to my feet and a light to my path." God doesn't promise to reveal the entire journey at once; instead, He illuminates each step as we take it. Faith is trusting that the next step will be shown, even if the entire road remains hidden.

Let me share a story from my own journey that captures this truth. When I finished my Bachelor's degree, I felt lost and uncertain about my next step. My family, with all the love and concern in the

40

world, offered their advice—one suggestion was to consider marriage. But I wasn't ready. Then, almost as if by divine appointment, three job offers appeared. I chose one and walked into it eagerly, excited to start a new chapter. On the first day, I was even given my own office. Yet, as I sat there, a quiet, unsettling voice seemed to ask, "Elsy, is this what I have prepared for you?"

For days, this voice persisted, a reminder that there was more to consider. I shared my discomfort with my family, and my father suggested that I continue my studies and pursue a Master's degree in India. It sounded reasonable, so we moved forward with the process, even paying the university fees. But on the journey home, that inner voice returned: "Elsy, did you ask Me if this is what I want for you?"

In search of clarity, I began praying more deeply, attending church, and spending time alone with God. Six months later, during a seemingly ordinary bus ride, a stranger sat next to me and, as if by divine insight, encouraged me to explore studying abroad. Her words felt like a door opening. After that conversation, I began researching and found that studying overseas would require a costly entrance exam. I prayed that if this were God's plan, He would provide the funds. Soon after, my sister met a woman whose daughter had been healed after our family prayed for her, and she insisted on giving us a gift. That gift covered the exam fees exactly. In that moment, I saw the purpose in what felt like waiting, confusion, and stillness. I realized that sometimes, discovering our path means surrendering our plans and trusting the One who knows the way forward.

Purpose in Every Step

The purpose is not something we only find at life's end or in grand accomplishments. It is in every small step, every moment of kindness, every prayer, and every act of faithfulness. Just as the roots of a tree anchor it to the ground, each step we take strengthens us in our walk with God. There's beauty in trusting that each part of our journey, even the parts that seem small or ordinary, contributes to fulfilling our divine purpose.

Nature teaches us not to rush. A seed doesn't push itself to bloom before its time, nor does a tree bear fruit out of season. In the same way, we are called to walk with God patiently, knowing that each season has its purpose. Even when we can't see the whole picture, as long as we walk with Him, we are living our purpose.

Discovering Our Place in the Vast Universe

Where do we fit in this vast universe? Just as each element in nature has its place and purpose in God's grand design, so do we. The universe may feel overwhelming in its vastness, but our purpose is crafted specifically for us by God Himself. In Christ, we're not wandering aimlessly; we are intricately woven into the fabric of creation, living out a purpose that is both personal and eternal.

CHAPTER 8:

TECHNOLOGY AND FAITH: DIFFERENT GENERATIONS, DIFFERENT MINDSETS

As the world evolves, so do the tools we use to navigate it. Just as nature reveals the intricate design of God's handiwork, technology has become a force that shapes our daily lives, offering new pathways for connection and understanding. With each generation, the way we engage with the world changes—how we communicate, learn, and grapple with questions of existence, purpose, and faith.

In this chapter, we explore how different generations have interacted with faith in an age of rapidly evolving technology. We'll see how these tools have shaped the way we search for our place in the universe and how we can bridge the gap between technological progress and spiritual grounding.

Every year, new technologies are developed, and with each passing century, mindsets shift to adapt to these advancements. I have a deep passion for technology—so much so that I've chosen to build my career in this field. I've had countless conversations with younger generations—Millennials and Gen Z—and found it fascinating to compare their perspectives on faith and technology to those of older generations like Gen X and Baby Boomers.

Generation X (1965–1980)

Millennials (1981–1996)

Generation Z (1997–2012)

These generational divides reflect not just differences in age but in worldview. My parents, part of Generation X, grew up in a time when technology was far less integrated into daily life. Their faith, based on my observations and statistics, was stronger and more deeply rooted, perhaps because there were fewer distractions. Although only a small percentage of Gen X identify as followers of Christ (around 30%), those who do seem to have a more solid foundation.

When I look at Millennials—my own generation—I notice a shift. Technology has become central to our lives, and while more Millennials (around 60%) have knowledge of Christ, their faith can be shaky. It's like a leaf swaying in the wind—fragile, easily influenced by the tides of culture and technology.

Generation Z, born with technology at their fingertips, seems to question faith more deeply. They know of God, but their faith often comes with doubt as they navigate a world of instant information and constant change.

But I'm not here to judge or criticize any generation. My point is this: no matter which generation we belong to, what culture we follow, or which country we call home, the essential question is whether we belong to the culture of God. Or, as I like to call it, the "Culture of Eden."

The Culture of Eden

The Culture of Eden is simple: it's just God and you—just like it was with Adam and Eve in the Garden of Eden. This culture focuses solely on God. Imagine a room with only two people: you and God. In that space, you can speak, and He listens, and He speaks, and you listen.

When we love someone, we naturally begin to adopt their characteristics, and the same is true when we are in the presence of God. As we spend time in this Eden-like relationship, we start to take on the nature of Jesus. There's no one else in that "garden" to influence us; it's just God, so naturally, we reflect His character.

The Bible says that God gives us the authority to call Him "Abba" or "Father." This reminds me of how, as a daughter, I inherited many things from my earthly father. Similarly, as God's children, we inherit all that He has. He is the Creator, and His creation belongs to us as well. Not only that, but His nature is also automatically instilled in us.

It's like installing software: the system asks if you'd like to accept the changes. Unless you say "yes," the installation won't proceed. Likewise, God offers His nature and everything He has, but He asks, "Do you want this transformation?" Unless we say "yes," we cannot inherit it.

So, it's up to us. He's ready to give everything—His love, His nature, His blessings—but it depends on how we answer. Entering the Garden of Eden isn't just a metaphor for a spiritual connection—it's a transformative experience that touches every aspect of your life. In this sacred space, you gain far more than just peace or reflection; you tap into a divine source of wisdom, growth, and purpose. Here's what you will find when you immerse yourself in the Culture of Eden:

The Secret of Eden: A Hidden Mystery in the Bible

The Garden of Eden, as portrayed in the Bible, is more than a physical place—it's a symbol, a mystery, and a profound reflection of humanity's relationship with God. Many read the story in Genesis as simply the beginning of creation, but within these verses lies the hidden secret of Eden, a mystery that invites us to explore deeper truths about our identity, our purpose, and our destiny in God.

1. The Garden as a Place of Divine Communion

The first secret of Eden is that it represents pure, unbroken communion with God. Before the fall, Adam and Eve walked with God in the cool of the day (Genesis 3:8). This wasn't just a physical stroll—it was an intimate connection, a shared life where nothing separated humanity from the Creator. Eden reveals the original design for humanity: a life lived in a direct, personal relationship with God.

In today's world, the secret of Eden can be reclaimed. Through prayer, worship, and stillness, we can return to that sacred place where God's voice is not distant but near. The real garden is not simply a historical location but a state of being, a return to divine intimacy.

.Picture a concert hall, but instead of instruments playing, there's silence—silence that allows you to hear God's whispers. In the Culture of Eden, this silence isn't empty; it's filled with the gentle voice of God guiding you. Without the distractions of the world, every whisper becomes clearer and every divine thought more profound. In this silence, you can hear the melodies of God's will, helping you make decisions, find peace, and live in harmony with His grace. Embracing moments of stillness opens up space for a deeper understanding of God's presence in your life.

2. The Tree of Life: Eternal Sustenance

One of the greatest mysteries hidden in Eden is the **Tree of Life** (Genesis 2:9). This tree symbolizes more than just eternal life; it represents the abundant, overflowing life that God intends for humanity. Eating from the Tree of Life would have kept Adam and

Eve in an eternal state of perfection, fully sustained by God's divine provision.

The secret here is that the Tree of Life is still accessible—not in the literal sense, but spiritually. Jesus, in many ways, becomes the fulfillment of the Tree of Life. In John 6:35, Jesus says, "I am the bread of life; whoever comes to me shall not hunger, and whoever believes in me shall never thirst." The true sustenance for our souls, the eternal nourishment we seek, is found in Christ. He is the secret source of life, offering what the Tree of Life in Eden promised: eternal communion with God.

The Tree Planted by the Water: As Jeremiah 17:8 beautifully illustrates, those who trust in the Lord are like trees planted by the waters. Their roots reach deep into the stream, drawing nourishment even during times of heat and drought. In the same way, when you root yourself in the Culture of Eden, you become like that tree. Your faith becomes steady and unshakable, even in the face of life's hardships. Your "leaves" always remain green—symbols of a vibrant, fruitful life that continues to grow, regardless of external circumstances. You bear fruit in all seasons, never fearing the future because your source of life is eternal and unyielding.

Rivers have a unique quality: they don't just flow in one direction; they branch out, creating new streams and tributaries. This is also true for the life lived in the Culture of Eden. When you align yourself with God's word instead of your feeling, your life doesn't just follow a single, predictable path. Instead, like a river, it branches out, giving rise to new opportunities, new directions, and new blessings. Each stream represents a fresh possibility—a new chance to grow, to love, to serve, or to learn. Your life, constantly branching out, creates a network of influence and impact, touching not only your own soul but also the lives of those around you.

Visualize a quiet, serene pool within the garden. As you look into the reflection pool, you see your reflection, but as you gaze deeper, you begin to see more than just yourself—you see the image of Christ. This reflection symbolizes self-examination, a reminder that as you grow in your relationship with God, you're being transformed to reflect His nature more and more. The pool shows that through your connection with God, you are constantly being reshaped, renewed, and made more like Him.

3. Eden as a Blueprint for Our Destiny

Eden was not just about the beginning of humanity—it is also a glimpse of the end. In the book of Revelation, the imagery of Eden reappears. The new heavens and new earth mirror the original paradise, with the Tree of Life once again at the center (Revelation 22:1-2). This cyclical pattern hints at a divine secret: Eden is not a lost dream but our ultimate destiny.

The secret of Eden is that it points to a future reality where we are fully restored to God's presence. In the same way that Adam and Eve were stewards of the garden, we are called to cultivate the spiritual "gardens" in our own lives. This restoration journey will lead us back to a state of harmony, where heaven and earth reunite and God's perfect will is accomplished

4. The Fall: A Door to Redemption

The expulsion of Adam and Eve from Eden might seem like the ultimate tragedy, but hidden within this moment is one of the Bible's greatest secrets: **the fall is the doorway to redemption**. By leaving the garden, humanity embarked on a journey where we would learn not only the weight of sin but also the depth of God's love and grace.

The secret is that Eden's loss paved the way for something even greater—**redemption through Christ**. Had humanity remained in

Eden, we would never have understood the boundless mercy of God. Through Christ's sacrifice, we are not just invited back to the Garden—we are invited to become co-heirs with Christ in God's kingdom (Romans 8:17). This is the hidden wisdom of Eden: that God's plan, even through human failure, was always aimed at greater glory and deeper love.

5. The Four Rivers: A Flow of Life and Purpose

In Genesis 2:10, we learn that a river flowed from Eden and divided into four headwaters, watering the entire land. The names of these rivers—Pishon, Gihon, Tigris, and Euphrates—carry symbolic meanings, often associated with increase, bursting forth, rapid flow, and fruitfulness.

The secret of the rivers is this: they represent the flow of divine purpose and provision in our lives. When you plant yourself in God's presence, your life becomes like these rivers—constantly flowing, never running dry, and spreading life wherever you go. Just as the rivers nourished the garden when we live in alignment with God's will, His blessings, wisdom, and favor flow into every area of our lives. Living in the Culture of Eden means living with purpose. Just as the rivers flow from Eden to water the garden and bring life to everything in their path, so too does your life flow outward, bringing grace, hope, and goodness wherever you go. Your actions, your words, and your faith all have the power to shape the world around you, creating ripples that extend far beyond what you can see. This is the flow of life in Eden—a life of constant motion, growth, and impact, rooted in the endless abundance of God's presence.

A River That Never Runs Dry: In Eden, there is no such thing as spiritual drought. The rivers that flow from this divine garden never stop moving. They nourish the land, sustain life, and bring forth abundance. When you plant your life in this Culture of Eden,

49

you are tapping into a source that will never run dry. In other words, you are planting your seeds by the River of Eden, sowing them in the fertile soil of divine abundance. Just as a river constantly flows, so will your life, continuously filled with new energy, creativity, and opportunities. Even in the driest of seasons—when challenges arise and hope seems scarce—the stream of life that flows from God ensures that your spirit remains nourished, your faith remains firm, and your purpose remains intact.

6. The Cherubim and the Flaming Sword: Guardians of the Secret

After Adam and Eve were expelled from Eden, God placed **cherubim and a flaming sword** to guard the way to the Tree of Life (Genesis 3:24). On the surface, this seems like a harsh punishment, but the deeper mystery here is protection, not rejection. The Tree of Life represents eternal life in an unfallen state, and without redemption, eternal life would have meant eternal separation from God.

The flaming sword symbolizes the refining power of God's truth and justice. It shows us that to return to the "secret garden" of God's presence, we must go through the refining fire of grace. The cherubim, often depicted as heavenly beings of great authority, represent the majesty and mystery of God's presence. The secret is that God, in His mercy, guards this sacred space but also invites us back to it through the purifying work of Christ.

7. Eden is Within You

The greatest secret of all is this: Eden is not a faraway place—it is within us. In Luke 17:21, Jesus tells us that "the kingdom of God is within you." The Garden of Eden, with all its abundance, peace, and connection to God, is not a lost reality but a present possibility.

When we align ourselves with God's will, cultivate a life of prayer, and seek His presence, we re-enter Eden. We live in that sacred space of divine relationship, where we walk with God, draw from the Tree of Life, and experience the rivers of His grace. The path reminds you that the journey itself is as valuable as the destination and that every experience along the way shapes your faith. This is the hidden truth of the Bible's first garden: Eden is not just where we came from—it's where we are meant to live every day through our faith.

Think of your relationship with God as a garden. In this garden, every intention you hold—whether it's a prayer, a thought, or a desire—is like a seed planted in the soil. In the Culture of Eden, each time you connect with God, you're tending to these seeds. As you nurture them with faith and patience, they bloom into beautiful flowers like love, joy, peace, and patience. Just as a gardener must dedicate time and effort to help plants grow, your spiritual growth requires care, patience, and trust in God's timing. The more you nurture your connection with God, the more you'll see the fruits of your intentions flourishing in your life.

An Eternal Flow Across Generations: The beauty of the Culture of Eden is that it transcends generations and mindsets. The flow of life in the Garden of Eden isn't bound by time or by the shifting cultures of humanity. It is a constant, available to everyone who seeks it, no matter their background, their age, or their stage in life. In the Culture of Eden, the sacred rhythm of life includes moments of prayer in the morning, gratitude throughout the afternoon, and reflection in the evening. As you live within the Culture of Eden, your transformation doesn't just affect you—it also influences those around you. Whether you are a part of Generation X, a Millennial, or Gen Z, the invitation remains the same: come to the rivers of Eden and be nourished. Here, the worries of the world fall away, and all that remains is the steady, eternal flow of God's love, grace, and purpose.

As we explore the intersection of technology and faith across generations, one truth emerges clearly: each generation, despite its different tools and evolving mindsets, is still engaged in the same timeless quest—the search for meaning and belonging in this vast universe.

Bridging Technology and Faith Across Generations:

From Generation X's grounded faith in a world less influenced by technology to Generation Z's skeptical yet curious engagement with spirituality in the digital age, we all wrestle with the same fundamental questions: Who am I? Where do I fit in this ever-expanding cosmos? And how do I balance the rapid pace of technological advancement with the deeper, eternal rhythms of spiritual life?

The challenge is not to choose between technology and faith but to let both inform and enhance our understanding of the divine. Just as technology connects us to each other, it can also be a bridge to deeper spiritual understanding if used wisely. However, the heart of the matter remains the same across all generations: our true belonging is found not in the devices we hold but in the hands of the Creator who holds us.

In the end, the "Culture of Eden" calls us back to simplicity, to a place of pure connection with God. As we advance through history, navigating the intricacies of technology and the complexities of life, the question isn't just how we use technology or how we view faith—it's whether we choose to return to that sacred space where we can find peace, purpose, and our true identity.

And perhaps, as we reflect on these generational shifts, we are invited to reconsider: are we allowing the noise of our modern world to drown out the whispers of divine truth? Or are we, like the rivers of Eden, flowing steadily towards the heart of our Creator, where we will ultimately find the answer to the question, "Where do I fit in this vast universe?"

CHAPTER 9:

PURPOSEFUL LIFE VS. PURPOSELESS LIFE

In the grand tapestry of existence, the question of purpose is one that echoes through every human heart. We often wonder, *Why am I here?* or *What am I meant to do with my life?* It's a question that seems simple but carries profound depth, influencing how we perceive ourselves, our decisions, and our place in the world. While society encourages us to pursue goals—wealth, status, family, success—there remains a deeper longing within us for something more. We crave a sense of purpose that transcends temporary achievements and connects us to a higher meaning.

In this chapter, we explore the difference between a life driven by purpose and one that feels purposeless. What makes our journey purposeful is not determined by how much we achieve or how grand our contributions seem but by recognizing the unique role we are meant to play in God's design. Just as no two people are alike, no two purposes are identical. We each have a calling shaped and refined by the hands of our Creator, and discovering this calling is what brings true fulfillment.

As we delve into the contrast between a life of purpose and a life without direction, I invite you to reflect on your own journey. Are you pursuing goals without understanding your deeper purpose, or have you found the unique role God has crafted for you? The purpose is not measured by human standards; it's a divine design that can only be fully realized through a relationship with Jesus Christ.

Building upon the previous chapter, we now understand that every living and non-living thing has a purpose. However, as human beings, we often fall into the trap of comparing our purpose with that of others, questioning whether our contribution is as significant. In this chapter, I want to explore the uniqueness of each person's purpose. One crucial point to remember is that purpose cannot be measured—it is neither small nor large. The purpose is not about size or status; it is about being unique and perfectly designed for you.

I have interviewed many adults and young people about their purpose in life. Some told me their purpose is simply to eat and sleep. Others said they wanted to become rich, while some mentioned that their purpose was to have a family and take care of them. A few said their goal is to travel the world, and others shared that they aspire to become scientists. The answers varied widely, reflecting different aspirations and desires.

I believe that everyone has their unique purpose, as well as their own life goals. But it's important to distinguish between goals and purpose. A **life goal** is a short-term process—once achieved, you can say you've accomplished something. However, the **purpose** is different. It is a long-term journey that aligns with our hope in Christ. Our purpose doesn't end until Jesus comes again or calls us home. Many of us confuse the two. Goals stem from our desires, while purpose comes from God's design. While Jesus can accompany us in achieving our goals, it's the journey of living out our purpose that I want to focus on here.

Just as goals vary from person to person, so does each individual's purpose, uniquely designed by God from the very beginning.

The House and the Broken Bricks: A Metaphor for Purpose

Let me offer an illustration to clarify this concept of unique purpose. Imagine someone constructing a house. The builder knows exactly how many bricks, steel rods, and other materials are needed to bring the design to life. At first glance, all the bricks may look identical—uniform in size and shape. However, as construction progresses, some bricks need to be chipped, shaped, or even broken to fit into specific spaces. These broken bricks, though they might seem damaged, serve a very special role in completing the structure. Without these specifically shaped bricks, the house wouldn't be built to plan—it would have gaps, be structurally weak, and could fall apart when storms come.

This image of broken bricks is a metaphor for our own lives. Some people may seem like perfectly shaped bricks, fitting neatly into place with little adjustment. But others—those of us who have been broken or shaped by life's challenges—are just as essential to the design. Our unique "brokenness" is often the key to fulfilling a purpose no one else can achieve. We each have a distinct role in the grand design of life, just as every brick has a specific place in the house.

1. God's Deliberate Design

Now, think about this from God's perspective. When He is shaping us for our unique purpose, He doesn't do it randomly. Unlike a builder who might choose bricks by chance, God chooses each of us deliberately. He knows everything about us—our strengths and weaknesses, how we react under pressure, how we cope with pain. He knows all these things, and yet He selects us, not because we're flawless, but because we are perfect for the purpose He has in mind. That's what makes us unique.

However, this process of being shaped can often be painful. Being molded for a specific purpose can involve challenges, setbacks, and suffering. But it's through these difficult times that we are prepared for our unique calling. Just like the brick must be broken to fit into its special place in the house, we might experience moments of brokenness that prepare us for something greater. Without these moments, our purpose wouldn't be fully realized.

To understand this even more deeply, imagine God as a master artist, painting a masterpiece that only He can see in its entirety. Just as an artist spends countless hours refining each detail, God paints our purpose with each experience—stroke by stroke, adding depth and meaning. Every challenge we face, every moment of joy or sorrow, becomes a brushstroke, shading and layering our lives. The shadows and highlights, the colors and textures, all blend to create something unique. We may not always see the complete picture, especially when life feels incomplete or challenging, but each stroke is essential to the final masterpiece.

God's artistry reflects His intentionality. Just as every color has a place in the painting, every moment of our lives fits uniquely within His larger vision. Even our imperfections, the parts of ourselves we might consider flaws, serve a purpose in His design. As the masterpiece unfolds, we come to understand that these details—the joys, the struggles, and the lessons—are part of a greater work of art that God is revealing through us.

2. The Music of Purpose

Imagine your life as a unique musical composition, a melody woven with purpose by the Master Composer. Every experience—both joyful and challenging—is like a note, carefully placed to create a symphony that resonates within God's grand design. Each high point is a crescendo, every sorrow a soft, lingering note.

Together, these moments blend to form a melody that is distinctly yours, a song that adds depth and color to God's vast creation.

Some seasons are gentle, like a soft lullaby, filled with peace and contentment. Other times brings intensity—a powerful movement of change and growth that stretches our limits. But each note, whether loud or soft, sorrowful or joyful, has a purpose. It builds upon the last, creating a harmony that wouldn't exist without every moment playing its part.

God, the Master Composer, orchestrates each rhythm with precision, blending our lives into a harmonious soundscape that is part of His greater plan. Just as an orchestra needs each instrument to contribute its sound, our lives add something vital to the world. Through all the highs and lows, our song unfolds, and even the dissonant chords are transformed into something beautiful as they resolve. And in the end, our lives become a symphony that speaks of God's purpose, a melody that reflects His love and design.

3. Seasons and Timing: Embracing the Rhythms of Purpose

Imagine your life unfolding like the changing seasons, each phase essential, each moment revealing a part of your purpose. Just as nature follows a rhythm that's beyond its control yet beautifully orchestrated, so do we journey through seasons that God has woven into His plan. Each season—whether marked by blossoming, waiting, or renewal—holds its own treasure, shaping us as we grow.

Flourish: Embracing Moments of Abundance

In seasons of flourishing, life feels alive with possibility, and purpose seems to burst forth like blossoms in spring. These are the times when our gifts come to light, when we feel ourselves moving in sync with what God created us to do. Think of this season as a time to marvel at how life unfolds when we step into our calling.

The beauty of flourishing lies not just in the outward results but in knowing we're growing into who God designed us to be.

Ask yourself: *Where do I see signs of flourishing in my life right now? How can I fully embrace and cultivate these areas with gratitude?*

Nourish: Strengthening the Roots Beneath

After the blooms of spring, there are quieter, unseen phases where we nourish the soil of our souls. These seasons teach us that true purpose requires deep roots, an inner strength that sustains us even in times of waiting. Just as a tree takes in nutrients from the earth to prepare for future growth, we, too, need seasons to be replenished, drawing wisdom, patience, and faith to fuel our journey. It is a time to invest in what can't be seen yet but will ultimately support every step forward.

Reflect: *What are the habits, people, or practices that nourish my spirit? How can I deepen my connection to them in this season?*

Cherish: Savoring the Present in All Its Beauty

Life's journey is not just about moving forward but also about cherishing the present and savoring the beauty of each moment. In seasons of cherishing, we pause and find meaning in what is, not just what's to come. These are the moments to celebrate small victories, acknowledge growth, and express gratitude for the path God has laid before us. Like a gardener pausing to admire the garden in bloom, we can look around and realize how far we've come and how much God has worked in our lives.

Consider: *What are the gifts in my life right now that I may have overlooked? How can I cherish and celebrate these blessings today?*

Rest: Trusting the Dormant Season

And then, there is rest—the winter of the soul. These are the seasons where purpose feels quiet, maybe even hidden. It's easy to feel restless, but winter has its own kind of purpose. Underneath the stillness, God is at work, restoring and preparing us for the future. Just as plants draw back into themselves to renew, we, too, need time to rest, to lay down our striving, and trust that God's timing is perfect. In these moments, we learn to surrender and trust in the unseen growth taking place beneath the surface.

Ponder: *Where am I being invited to rest and trust in God's unseen work? What would it look like to release control and let Him prepare me for this season?*

In every season—flourishing, nourishing, cherishing, and resting—God's hand is upon us, guiding us gently, inviting us to grow into the fullness of His purpose. These rhythms teach us that purpose is not a single destination but a journey where each phase matters. So, as we walk through these seasons, may we trust in God's perfect timing and let each moment, each season, shape us in the ways only He can design.

4. Purpose Beyond Comparison: The Weaver's Loom

Imagine a master weaver at a grand loom, carefully selecting threads of every color, texture, and strength. Each thread may look simple on its own, but as the weaver pulls it through, it becomes an essential part of a beautiful, intricate tapestry. Some threads are bright and bold, catching the eye immediately. Others are subtle, delicate, and woven in the background. Yet every single thread— bright or muted, thick or fine—has a place and purpose in the design, a role only it can fulfill. If a single thread were missing, the whole tapestry would lack harmony.

In the same way, each of our lives is a unique thread in the tapestry of God's design. Your purpose isn't meant to compete with others, nor to mimic the role of another thread, but to contribute in the way only you can. When we compare our journey to someone else's, it's like pulling a thread from the tapestry, weakening its beauty and integrity. Just as each thread is necessary to complete the picture, your purpose is essential to the whole, adding richness and depth that no other thread could bring.

Consider this: a single golden thread may look different from a bold red one, but each adds value to the masterpiece. Without the delicate gold, there might be no shimmer; without the red, no vibrance. If the red thread looked down upon itself for not being as fine as the gold, or if the gold envied the red's boldness, they would lose sight of the beauty they create together. So it is with our lives—no purpose is superior to another, no path more valuable. Each life, each purpose, is woven into a larger vision that is beautiful only when every unique part is present.

Think of your own journey as that one-of-a-kind thread. Your experiences, talents, strengths, and even struggles are fibers woven together by God's hand, adding to a picture far beyond what you can see from where you stand. Sometimes, our purpose may seem hidden, perhaps part of a quieter background that doesn't draw immediate attention. Yet the strength of a tapestry lies in these foundational threads as much as in the bold strokes.

The beauty of the weaver's work reminds us to appreciate our own place without looking sideways and to trust that God has chosen each thread intentionally. Just as the golden thread never questions its worth because it isn't red, we, too, can rest in the knowledge that our purpose, no matter how different, adds something beautiful and irreplaceable to the world.

So as you walk your path, remember that you are a carefully chosen thread woven with care into a masterpiece only God can fully see. There is no need to compare or compete, for in the weaver's design, every thread matters, every purpose is priceless, and every life is indispensable to the tapestry as a whole.

Personal Testimony: Discovering My Purpose

At this point, I want to share a personal story. After completing my Bachelor's degree, my parents began searching for a future husband for me, according to Indian culture, where parents often arrange marriages (Partially, this culture is dying). Especially for daughters, there's an expectation to marry at a certain age. At 23, my parents felt it was the right time, but I didn't want to get married then. I didn't want to directly tell my parents, as they might feel I was disobeying them.

Instead, I turned to Jesus in prayer. I would wake up in the middle of the night, praying for Him to reveal my purpose and guide my path. At that time, I felt like I was being pushed into the same cycle of life that everyone else was following: marriage, children, and family life. While I eventually wanted these things, I knew 23 wasn't the right time for me. Miraculously, Jesus blocked every person who came forward as a potential match. He heard my prayers.

The reason I'm sharing this personal story is to highlight that **God's purpose in our lives never changes**, even if our circumstances or desires do. Life may change, people may change, and situations may shift, but God's purpose remains constant, as He has designed it for each individual. Even when we might stray due to our stubbornness or disobedience, His purpose stands firm.

Take the story of Joseph from the Bible as an example. At 18, Joseph saw a dream of his future. But it wasn't until he was 30 that he became a leader in Egypt. Along the way, he faced numerous temptations, persecutions, and setbacks. It's possible that at some point, Joseph may have even forgotten God's promise to him. But despite walking through the valley of hardship, **God never forgot His purpose for Joseph**, and that same truth applies to us.

Pain, Purpose, and the Role of Jesus

Even though we are called to be unique, we cannot fulfill our potential without Jesus in our lives. He is the one who helps us through the process, who gives our lives flavor and meaning, and who ensures that our purpose—however it may appear to us or others—fits perfectly into His greater plan. Only through Jesus can we live out our true potential and find completeness in the vast design of life.

By recognizing that your purpose is not something that can be measured or compared but something uniquely molded by God, you can embrace the process of becoming who you are meant to be. Pain, challenges, and even moments of doubt are part of that journey, but with Jesus by your side, you will see that your unique role is both valuable and essential to the world around you.

Purpose is not about accomplishments or goals—it's about fulfilling God's design for your life. The world may change, but the purpose God created for you will never fade. Even if you lose sight of your purpose in moments of trial, remember that the One who designed you in your mother's womb has never lost sight of it. Keep Jesus close, and He will reveal the full beauty of the life He has planned for you.

CHAPTER 10:

THE VOID WITHOUT PURPOSE

There is a deep, undeniable longing in every human soul—a search for significance, for something greater than ourselves. This search is universal, transcending cultures, beliefs, and backgrounds. Yet, as we navigate this quest for purpose, we find that what we choose to believe in shapes the course of our lives. For many, this pursuit is driven by the need to understand why we are here and what we are meant to do.

Without Jesus, however, this search for purpose becomes clouded and ultimately empty. We may attempt to fill the void with personal achievements, science, or the teachings of other spiritual leaders, but these solutions, while perhaps offering temporary satisfaction, fail to address the deeper need for eternal purpose. The human soul was not made for temporal things—it was designed to be filled with something eternal.

This chapter will explore the question of purpose from various perspectives and ultimately guide us to the conclusion that true purpose is found only in Christ. Without Him, we remain like a vessel without a destination—adrift, searching, but never truly arriving. It invites us to examine what we're filling our souls with. Are we feeding our lives with things that will lead us toward true purpose, or are we drifting aimlessly, trying to fill the void with things that will never truly satisfy? The answer to a meaningful life lies not just in what we believe but in who we believe in. Only in Jesus can we find the purpose that our souls long for.

One of the central points in understanding life's purpose is the realization that without Jesus, life is ultimately purposeless. To explore this further, I engaged in conversations with several of my non-Christian friends to gain their perspectives on the purpose of life. I didn't do this to judge them but to understand different viewpoints and explore the contrast in beliefs. When I asked about their understanding of purpose, many shared their belief in deities such as Vishnu, Shiva, and others. From this, I realized that while they believed in purpose, their understanding was tied to a different view of divinity.

Then, I asked a different question to friends who identified as atheists—those who don't believe in any god. Their answers pointed to science as their guiding force and the source of purpose. What became clear to me was that even those who deny the existence of God still seek purpose in something. Whether it's science, philosophy, or some other belief system, they fill their lives with something to anchor themselves.

This realization led me to an important conclusion: as human beings, we need to believe in something to find purpose in life. Our souls are not meant to be empty or directionless. We are always in search of meaning, and the question is not *whether* we believe but *what* we choose to believe in. Our soul craves fulfillment, and what we feed it determines whether we experience a purposeful life or a purposeless one.

As Christians, we believe that the truth of God's Word fills and nourishes our souls. The Bible tells us that *"the truth shall set you free"* (John 8:32). This truth, found in Jesus Christ, is what gives our lives purpose and meaning. Without it, life becomes an aimless search for fulfillment in things that cannot truly satisfy.

Echoes of Emptiness: When Life Loses Its Core

What does it mean to live a life disconnected from true purpose? Scripture uses powerful metaphors that reveal how a purposeless life, no matter how full it may appear, lacks the essence that makes it meaningful and fulfilling. These images from the Bible show that without God as our source, life becomes a hollow version of what it was meant to be.

A Tree Without Fruit: In the Gospel of Matthew, Jesus speaks about a tree that is nurtured and cared for but produces no fruit. Imagine a tree that grows tall and wide, with green leaves and strong branches, yet year after year, it bears nothing. No fruit to nourish, no seeds to spread new life, and no contribution to the ecosystem it inhabits. Such a tree is cut down and discarded because it fails to fulfill the purpose for which it was created. Likewise, when we live without Jesus, our lives may seem healthy and vibrant on the surface—we may be busy, successful, or even admired by others— but spiritually, we are barren. A life without Jesus is one of striving but not achieving the deep, lasting impact that God intended for us. Spiritual fruit is the evidence of God working in and through us, and without Him, we are merely existing, not truly living.

A Lamp Without Oil: In the parable of the ten virgins, Jesus talks about lamps that run out of oil, leaving them unable to provide light. Picture a lamp crafted with care, designed to shine brightly in the darkness. Yet, without oil, its potential remains unrealized—it cannot light the way for others or even for itself. In this metaphor, the oil represents the Holy Spirit, the divine presence that fuels our lives and gives us purpose. Without the Holy Spirit, we lack the inner spark that enables us to reflect the light of God's truth. No matter how elaborate the design of the lamp, without oil, it is just an empty vessel. Similarly, without the presence of God in our lives, we might have great talents, plans, or ambitions, but they fail to shine with the light of divine purpose. The light within us goes dim, leaving us wandering in the shadows of a life that is never fully illuminated by God's vision for us.

A River Without Water: A river, by its very nature, is meant to flow and bring life to everything in its path. But a dry riverbed, cracked and barren, no longer serves its purpose. Imagine walking along a once-vibrant riverbank, now dusty and desolate, unable to provide the refreshment or sustenance it once did. A river without water is a symbol of potential without power, of motion without movement. This is what life without Jesus looks like—empty, disconnected from the true source of life. We may go through the motions of living, but without Christ flowing through us like living water, we are unable to nourish others or even ourselves. Just as a dry riverbed is incapable of sustaining life, a soul without Jesus lacks the vital force that makes it purposeful, fruitful, and life-giving.

Salt Without Flavor: Jesus also uses the metaphor of salt that has lost its flavor, explaining that such salt is no longer good for anything. Salt is a simple yet profound element—it preserves, enhances, and brings out the best in what it touches. Imagine salt that has lost its ability to do what it was created to do; it becomes nothing more than a useless, bland mineral. Salt without flavor is not just ineffective—it's irrelevant. In the same way, when we live apart from Jesus, we lose our purpose, our uniqueness, and the ability to impact the world around us. Our lives were designed to preserve goodness, to enhance the lives of others, and to reflect the glory of God. But without Jesus, we lose that essence. We become like flavorless salt—our actions may continue, but they no longer have the power to preserve or transform.

A Vessel without Water: Imagine a beautifully crafted clay pot meticulously shaped and designed with purpose. It has the strength to hold water and the beauty to enhance any space. But an empty pot cannot quench thirst, no matter how skillfully it is crafted. A life without Jesus is like this vessel—built with potential but lacking the living water that makes it truly useful. We may possess talents, wealth, or charisma, yet without the life-giving Spirit of God filling us, we remain empty. The potential is there, but the true purpose is unrealized. It's only when God fills us with His Spirit that we become vessels overflowing with life, able to pour out His love, wisdom, and compassion to others.

A ody without Breath: In Genesis, God breathed life into humanity, transforming dust into a living being. Without breath, the body is mere clay. It has the appearance of life but lacks its animating essence. In the same way, a life without divine purpose is like a body without breath. We may go through the motions—working, achieving, striving—but we're simply existing rather than living. The purpose of our lives is not just to move or to survive but to be alive in a deeper, spiritual sense. Jesus said, "I have come that they may have life, and have it to the full" (John 10:10). A life without God's purpose is like a body without breath: it lacks the spark, the vitality, the essence of true life.

A Branch without Connection: In John 15, Jesus speaks of Himself as the vine and His followers as the branches. "Apart from Me, you can do nothing," He says, reminding us that our purpose is deeply rooted in our connection to Him. Picture a branch broken off from a tree—though it may look green and vibrant for a while, it will eventually wither, for it has lost its source of nourishment. When we are separated from God, we may have moments of joy or achievement, but without the sustaining power of Jesus, these are temporary and will eventually fade. A branch is only fruitful when it abides in the vine, and similarly, our lives bear lasting fruit only when we remain connected to Christ. Without Him, we're like severed branches, capable of a short-lived appearance of life but ultimately unable to bear true, lasting fruit.

A House without a Foundation: Jesus tells the story of two houses: one built on sand and the other on rock. When the storms came, the house on the sand collapsed, while the one on the rock stood firm. A purposeless life is like a house built on sand; it may look sturdy and beautiful on the outside, but when challenges arise, it crumbles. Many people build their lives on unstable foundations—career success, relationships, personal achievements—but these can shift like sand. The true purpose is found in a life anchored to Jesus, the unshakable Rock. Without this foundation, everything we build is vulnerable to collapse. But with Christ as our foundation, our lives become resilient, able to withstand the storms and trials that come our way.

Each of these metaphors reveals a deeper truth about what it means to live disconnected from the purpose for which we were created. A purposeless life is not simply a life without goals or ambitions—it's a life cut off from the source of meaning, left empty despite appearances. Only through a relationship with Jesus Christ do we find the life-giving water, the spiritual fruit, the light, and the flavor that make life truly meaningful.

The Search for Fulfillment: In conversations with people from diverse backgrounds—whether they place their faith in science, another belief system, or their own understanding—I noticed a shared theme: a search for something deeper, a sense of fulfillment that reaches beyond day-to-day life. Beneath all individual beliefs lies a universal longing, a void in the soul each person tries to fill. This search is not unique to Christianity; it's a part of the human experience. We are all wired with a need for purpose, for something greater than ourselves. But as a Christian, I have come to realize that only Jesus Christ can fill this void. He is not just one answer among many; He is the source of all truth and the key to discovering our true purpose.

Chasing Mirage Fulfillment: The world presents countless distractions and false purposes, each promising fulfillment. Wealth, success, status, and personal happiness are often held up as the ultimate treasures of a "well-lived life." Yet, these pursuits, captivating as they may be, often feel like drinking from a mirage—offering flashes of satisfaction that quickly fade, leaving us thirstier than before. We may fill our cups with worldly pursuits, but the soul remains unsatisfied, longing for something that lasts.

True fulfillment—the kind that quenches the deepest thirst within us—comes when we align ourselves with the purpose God designed for us. We weren't created to chase fleeting pleasures or worldly achievements but were crafted for a timeless purpose that reflects God's eternal plan. This purpose is fully realized only when we surrender our lives to Jesus, entrusting our dreams to His hands and trusting that His vision surpasses anything we could imagine for ourselves.

The Lighthouse and the Anchored Ship: A life with purpose is like a ship anchored near a lighthouse, while a life without purpose drifts through dark waves, tossed by every wind of uncertainty. Without a lighthouse to guide it and an anchor to hold it steady, a ship wanders aimlessly, never reaching the shore. Similarly, when we root ourselves in the temporary—success, approval, self-sufficiency—we remain adrift, constantly searching for stability but finding none. Yet, when we entrust our lives to Jesus, He becomes the lighthouse that guides us through the fog and the anchor that holds us steady in turbulent seas. In Him, we find direction and security, no longer tossed by every passing tide.

The Incomplete Symphony: Imagine a symphony played by an orchestra, each instrument essential to the composition. Now, imagine one key instrument, like the strings, is missing. The music becomes incomplete, hollow, and missing its intended depth. A life without purpose is like this symphony—lacking harmony, richness, and fullness. Each of us was created to play a unique role in God's divine composition, and without His direction, we lose the melody we were meant to contribute. Surrendering to God brings us into harmony, creating beauty we couldn't achieve alone.

The Lighthouse and the Fog: Purpose is like a lighthouse in the fog—a fixed point drawing us forward even when the path is unclear. The world can feel like a dense fog filled with distractions and diversions, each promising happiness. But only the lighthouse, constant and unwavering, can guide us home. Purpose, like the lighthouse, is a light more profound than any temporary achievement, something that calls us beyond ourselves. When we place our faith in Jesus, He becomes our guiding light through life's uncertainties, calling us toward a purpose as steady as the lighthouse itself. He provides clarity in the fog of life, giving us direction and meaning when everything else is unclear.

The Woven Tapestry: Imagine our lives as threads in a vast, intricate tapestry. Each thread may seem ordinary on its own, unremarkable in color and unclear in purpose. But woven together with others, these individual strands create a stunning masterpiece. God, as the master weaver, takes each of our lives—our gifts, experiences, and struggles—and weaves them into a design far greater than we can see from our limited perspective. Our purpose is uniquely ours, chosen by God for a specific place in His tapestry. When we surrender to His design, we see the full picture and the beauty we couldn't have achieved alone.

The Endless Well: Imagine a well with an unending source, reaching deep into the earth and never running dry. True fulfillment, like the water from this well, flows not from our efforts but from an eternal source. Jesus offers Himself as this well of living water, filling us from within so that we never thirst again. While the world's pursuits are like empty cisterns—filled and emptied over and over—Jesus offers a source that continually replenishes. He doesn't satisfy us temporarily; He transforms us into wells of living water ourselves, overflowing with purpose, joy, and peace that reaches those around us.

Anchoring in Eternal Purpose

In the end, the difference between a life filled with purpose and one without is not about what we accomplish but in whom we place our trust. When we seek to anchor our lives in temporary things, we find ourselves drifting, always in search of something stable. But when we anchor ourselves in Jesus, we find a purpose that is both unshakable and eternal. A life anchored in Christ becomes a wellspring of love, joy, and peace, overflowing with meaning and grounded in truth.

True purpose isn't something we achieve on our own; it is a gift we receive through surrender. By yielding to God's guidance, we stop wandering aimlessly and find our place in a divine plan far beyond our imagination. In Jesus, we discover that our lives are neither random nor insignificant; they are threads in an eternal tapestry, each one essential to the whole. We become vessels of His love, lights that never dim, and trees that bear fruit through every season.

Fulfillment is not found in seeking something external; it is in embracing the life God designed us to live. It is a journey that brings us closer to the heart of our Creator, a journey that transforms us from within, making us everything He created us to be.

CHAPTER 11:

NAVIGATING DOUBTS AND DISCOVERING PURPOSE

In the context of my book, *Where Do I Fit in the Vast Universe?* Chapter 10 delves into the inevitable doubts and questions that arise when contemplating one's place in such an expansive cosmos. When we gaze at the stars or reflect on the complexity of existence, it's natural to wonder about our own significance. In the search for meaning, doubt often becomes the first step in questioning who we are and where we belong. Rather than viewing doubt as an obstacle, however, we can understand it as a vital part of our journey toward deeper self-awareness and spiritual discovery.

This chapter will explore how doubt is not something to fear but rather a powerful tool for personal growth. Many doubts stem from the apparent contradiction between faith and reason, but these uncertainties can be addressed in ways that reveal how faith and logic can actually work in harmony. By embracing doubt, we can challenge ourselves to examine long-held beliefs, refine our understanding, and come to a more profound and grounded perspective.

In the vastness of the universe, one of the most profound inquiries centers on personal significance—*"Why am I here?"* or *"What does it mean to exist?"* Other questions may include, *"How does our experience shape our understanding of purpose?"* or *"In what ways can faith influence our sense of significance?"* We also grapple with questions like *"How do we reconcile feelings of insignificance with the desire to make a meaningful impact?"* These questions prompt deep existential reflections that naturally arise as we try to understand the meaning of life and our role in it.

Throughout this chapter, we will explore how personal purpose is influenced by both external elements, such as the vastness of the physical universe, and internal forces, like faith, values, and personal experiences.

Doubt inevitably accompanies these big questions, placing us in a unique position to seek answers. However, it's important to recognize whether we are genuinely seeking truth or if we have already been influenced by misguided beliefs that we mistakenly label as truth. It's perfectly normal to have questions that stretch beyond our imagination as long as we continue to seek with an open mind and heart.

In this chapter, we will explore how doubt can be transformed from a source of fear into a catalyst for personal and spiritual growth. We will examine the role doubt plays in shaping our understanding of faith, purpose, and significance in the universe. Readers will learn how to navigate the seeming contradictions between faith and reason and how to find harmony between the two. Ultimately, this chapter will provide insights into how we can approach our most profound questions with courage, seeking answers that deepen our sense of purpose and help us find our place in the vast universe.

Understanding the Roots of Doubt

Doubt is a feeling almost everyone faces at some point, but to truly understand it, we must look closely at how it forms. Doubt often arises from three main sources: **(1) ingrained false beliefs or "wrong inputs," (2) unanswered questions, and (3) lack of understanding**. Each of these roots of doubt affects us differently, but they all contribute to a cycle of fear and uncertainty. By examining these three parameters, we can better understand the complexity of doubt and learn how to address it constructively.

1. Ingrained False Beliefs – The "Wrong Inputs"

The most challenging form of doubt stems from false beliefs we've held onto over time, which become deeply ingrained "truths" in our minds. These might be incorrect perceptions about ourselves, our abilities, or even our purpose. The problem with these false beliefs is that, over time, they are stored in our mental "database" as if they were absolute truths. We build our thoughts, emotions, and actions around these beliefs, which form a foundation that is shaky and unreliable.

For instance, imagine someone who has always believed they are unworthy or inadequate. This person might have received this message from an early age—perhaps through the words of others, past mistakes, or social pressures. Over time, they internalize this perception, even if it isn't true. Now, whenever they face a new challenge or opportunity, this sense of unworthiness resurfaces as doubt, holding them back from fully engaging with life's possibilities.

This parameter is especially tricky because it's like trying to build on a foundation made of sand. When we store these wrong inputs as if they were truths, we unconsciously allow them to shape our actions and responses. They become self-fulfilling; believing you're unworthy makes you hesitant to pursue what you want, leading to a cycle of doubt. Breaking free requires intense self-reflection and a willingness to confront and replace these false beliefs with genuine truths. But doing so is difficult because our minds resist letting go of ideas we've held onto for so long.

2. Unanswered Questions

Doubt often emerges from questions that seem to lack clear or immediate answers, especially the profound, life-shaping ones we carry: "What is my purpose?" "Why does suffering exist?" or "What does faith truly mean?" Such questions unsettle us because they confront the unknown, an area where human understanding often falls short. We naturally crave answers, yet some of these deeper questions linger unanswered, and in that lingering, doubt arises.

However, the presence of these unanswered questions isn't inherently negative. They serve as invitations to search for understanding, which, in itself, can be a path toward growth. Seeking answers to deep questions draws us into experiences, conversations, and reflections that often add layers of meaning to our lives, even if we don't find a concrete answer. For example, when someone is driven to explore their purpose, they might try new things, engage in meaningful work, or seek spiritual guidance. The doubt stirred by unanswered questions becomes a catalyst, encouraging us to look beyond our immediate understanding and embrace the journey of searching.

While some answers may take time or may even remain mysterious, the act of searching strengthens our resilience and often leads us closer to truths we hadn't considered. Over time, embracing these unanswered questions with curiosity rather than frustration can turn doubt into a path of discovery, where each step forward brings new insights and, perhaps, a deepening of faith.

3. Lack of Understanding

Doubt also takes hold when we face things we don't yet understand or when we lack clarity about a situation. This can include challenges that feel too big, responsibilities we don't feel prepared for, or even spiritual concepts that seem beyond our grasp. A lack of understanding can leave us feeling small or inadequate, leading to self-doubt and a reluctance to move forward.

Imagine someone encountering a new chapter in life, such as a challenging career path or a difficult spiritual question. Not having the understanding needed to feel confident, they may start to question their abilities, decisions, or even their faith. This form of doubt is deeply uncomfortable because it forces us to confront our own limitations, pushing us toward an unknown that feels intimidating.

Yet, this lack of understanding also invites us to grow. Instead of allowing it to paralyze us, we can choose to seek out the knowledge, skills, or insight we need. Reaching out to mentors, immersing ourselves in learning, or turning to faith for guidance can fill these gaps, transforming doubt into a stepping stone toward greater clarity. Embracing doubt in this context helps us develop the humility to learn and the courage to pursue deeper truths, ultimately leading us to a place of understanding that strengthens our faith and self-belief.

Circular Economy of Doubt and Fear

Doubt doesn't operate in isolation; it tends to generate emotions that reinforce and expand its influence. One of the most powerful companions of doubt is fear. Together, they create a circular economy, a cycle where one fuels the other, generating more anxiety, avoidance, and, ultimately, more doubt. This circular pattern of doubt and fear is self-reinforcing—doubts lead to fear, fear breeds more doubts, and the cycle continues, each round making it harder to break free.

Imagine a child who has made a mistake, perhaps breaking something valuable in the household. The child's first response might be a pang of doubt—doubt about how their parents will react, doubt about their own worth, or fear of punishment. This initial doubt quickly transforms into fear: the child fears getting in trouble or facing disappointment from their parents. Rather than facing up to the mistake, the child tries to hide it, perhaps by covering it up or even lying to avoid punishment.

But this avoidance doesn't end the problem; it compounds it. The child now has the weight of both the initial mistake and the dishonesty, leading to a stronger sense of anxiety. Each time they think about the hidden mistake, they experience fresh fear of being discovered, which feeds back into their original doubt—this time even stronger, as they now doubt their own honesty or sense of self. This circular process reinforces itself with every attempt to avoid the initial mistake, leading to a loop where doubt breeds fear, and fear deepens doubt.

This circular economy of doubt and fear operates in our lives in various ways, extending beyond childhood. When we face doubts in areas like our abilities, relationships, or faith, the first response is often to fear what might happen if these doubts turn out to be true. This fear then drives avoidance—we avoid challenging our beliefs or confronting the unknown. But rather than reducing doubt, avoidance magnifies it. Like the child hiding their mistake, we bury our uncertainties instead of addressing them, allowing them to build and recycle back into new doubts.

This cycle is particularly hard to break because it's self-sustaining. Each element feeds the other, creating an ongoing loop that limits our ability to confront or resolve the doubt at its source. The more we allow doubt and fear to avoid facing an issue directly, the more our anxiety grows, keeping us trapped in a mindset where doubt overshadows confidence and fear outweighs courage.

Breaking out of this circular economy requires disrupting the cycle—by choosing to confront, rather than avoid, the initial doubt. This could mean acknowledging our feelings of fear, seeking reassurance, or actively seeking answers to our questions. In this way, the energy of doubt and fear can be transformed from a self-sustaining cycle into a constructive journey toward growth and understanding.

Breaking the Cycle: Moving from Fear to Growth

Breaking free from the circular economy of doubt and fear requires a conscious shift—from letting doubts feed fear to using them as stepping stones toward growth. Each form of doubt—whether rooted in false beliefs, unanswered questions, or lack of understanding—requires a unique approach to transform fear into a source of strength and clarity. By addressing each type directly, we can begin to navigate doubt as a journey of personal and spiritual growth.

1. Overcoming False Beliefs: Self-Reflection and Seeking Truth

False beliefs are some of the most difficult doubts to overcome because they often operate beneath our awareness, rooted in assumptions we've accepted as "truths" over time. To break the cycle of doubt stemming from these beliefs, the first step is to challenge and reframe them through intentional self-reflection.

Start by identifying the beliefs you hold about yourself that might not be true or helpful. Ask yourself: *"What beliefs about myself or the world am I holding onto, and where did these come from?"* Often, false beliefs arise from past experiences, mistakes, or negative feedback from others, which we internalize as truth. By questioning their validity, we can start to separate assumptions from reality.

The next step is actively seeking truth. This could mean replacing negative self-talk with affirmations grounded in reality, finding supportive and honest friends who can give objective feedback, or spending time in prayer or meditation to seek guidance. This process of reframing takes time, but with persistence, you can replace deeply ingrained assumptions with beliefs that are authentic and uplifting, helping you grow in confidence and diminish the doubt that stems from falsehoods.

2. Addressing Unanswered Questions: Cultivating Curiosity Through Faith

Unanswered questions can often create doubt by confronting us with the unknown. But rather than seeing these questions as obstacles, we can approach them with a mindset of faith-filled curiosity, trusting that God is present even in the midst of uncertainty. Instead of fearing unanswered questions, consider them as invitations from God to deepen your understanding of Him and His purpose for you.

Begin by embracing your questions as opportunities for spiritual growth. When questions about purpose, faith, or the mysteries of life arise, view them as ways to draw closer to God. In the Bible, figures like David, Job, and Paul asked profound, sometimes difficult, questions of God—questions about suffering, purpose, and the nature of faith. Their questions didn't separate them from God; instead, they led to deeper insights and strengthened their relationship with Him. A similar approach can help us grow closer to God, even when the answers aren't immediate.

In your search for understanding, spend time in prayer, bringing your questions to God directly. Ask Him to reveal wisdom through His Word. Consider using passages from the Bible as a starting point, allowing Scripture to offer guidance and perspective on your questions. Passages like James 1:5 remind us that "if any of you lacks wisdom, let him ask of God, who gives to all liberally and without reproach, and it will be given to him." This promise assures us that God welcomes our questions and will provide insight into His timing.

Additionally, engaging in quiet reflection can be invaluable. Through journaling, meditation on Scripture, and spending time in nature, you can invite God to speak to your heart, revealing insights that may not come through words alone. Embracing these unanswered questions as part of your faith journey can turn doubt into an opportunity for closeness with God, strengthening your faith as you wait for His direction.

Remember that God often uses these questions to deepen our understanding and grow our trust. Although some answers may take time, leaning on your faith throughout the search transforms doubt from an obstacle into a meaningful path toward a closer relationship with God.

3. Addressing Lack of Understanding: Seeking Wisdom and Clarity Through Faith

A lack of understanding can create doubt by highlighting the gap between where we are and where we want to be, whether in our faith, knowledge, or abilities. But instead of letting this gap breed uncertainty, we can embrace it as an invitation to grow closer to God, trusting that He is the ultimate source of wisdom. When faced with confusion, we can turn to Him for guidance, knowing that He promises to give clarity to those who seek it.

The first step is to bring this need for understanding to God in prayer, asking for His insight in specific areas where you feel uncertain. Proverbs 2:6 reminds us, "For the Lord gives wisdom; from His mouth come knowledge and understanding." This promise means that we can trust God to illuminate our path, providing direction as we seek His wisdom.

If certain tasks or challenges feel overwhelming, ask God for guidance and strength to navigate them. Take practical steps, such as breaking down tasks into manageable parts or approaching each task with patience and diligence. Through faith, we can face these tasks not alone but with the confidence that God will empower us along the way. Remember that Scripture encourages us to pursue knowledge with humility, trusting that growth often comes in small, steady steps rather than in sudden revelations.

Studying Scripture and spending time with God's Word can also provide profound clarity in areas that feel confusing. When we approach the Bible as a guide, we can find answers that offer both spiritual and practical insight. Reflecting on passages relevant to our struggles, praying for guidance, and immersing ourselves in God's wisdom helps bridge the gap between doubt and faith.

As you grow in understanding through these steps, remember that clarity often requires patience. Just as seeds need time to grow, God often teaches us gradually, leading us step by step. Embracing this process allows us to transform areas of confusion into opportunities for spiritual growth, strengthening our confidence in both our abilities and in God's unwavering guidance.

4. Building Faith as a Foundation

Faith acts as a firm foundation—a grounding force that doesn't seek to eliminate doubt entirely but to redefine it. In many ways, faith transforms doubt from a wall blocking our progress into a bridge that leads us to greater growth, resilience, and understanding. When we embrace faith as our foundation, we begin to see doubt not as a threat but as a tool that strengthens our journey.

Consider doubt as a river running between where we are and where we long to be: a place of peace, clarity, and fulfillment. Without faith, we're often left standing at the riverbank, staring across at the other side, unsure of how to reach it. Faith becomes the bridge that allows us to cross, providing support and structure even when we feel uncertain. Each plank of the bridge—trust, patience, perseverance—reinforces our steps forward, inviting us to walk over our doubts rather than being stopped by them.

Faith doesn't remove the challenges of doubt but rather equips us to face them. As we cross this bridge, we may encounter moments where the journey feels shaky, where doubts stir up old fears. Yet each step across is also a step deeper into resilience, showing us that faith is not fragile. Faith doesn't crumble under doubt; it adapts, grows stronger, and teaches us that trust in God can support us even when answers remain unclear. This bridge of faith shows us that doubt need not block us from progress—it is simply part of the journey.

In this way, faith redefines doubt. Rather than a barrier, doubt becomes a means of developing courage, patience, and humility. Faith invites us to turn our uncertainty into a source of insight, leading us to question, explore, and ultimately grow closer to God. When faith is our foundation, doubt can serve as a stepping stone on the bridge of growth. And with each step we take, we build a relationship with God that is more resilient, more compassionate, and more understanding.

By transforming doubt into an opportunity to walk in faith, we learn that true growth comes from relying on God as the solid ground beneath us, guiding us across whatever rivers of doubt we may face.

Doubt as a Gateway to Purpose

In the vast tapestry of life, doubt isn't a barrier; it's a beckoning doorway—a gateway inviting us to step beyond the familiar and uncover the depth of our unique purpose. When doubt arises, it doesn't close off possibility; rather, it signals the start of a journey, leading us to uncover hidden truths about ourselves, our faith, and the world around us. To doubt is to be invited into something larger, something that can shape us in ways we never anticipated.

Imagine doubt as a mysterious passageway in a great, ancient library. You find yourself drawn to a door, slightly ajar, through which a warm light spills out. As you approach, there's a sense of the unknown, yet, something compels you to step forward. Each step past this doorway represents a question, a curiosity, a willingness to explore. Though you may feel unprepared, each moment spent in this vast room, exploring the "books" of your own questions and curiosities, reveals something precious: a deeper understanding, a layer of truth you couldn't have seen without first being open to doubt.

In this vast and mysterious universe, doubt acts as a compass, guiding us through our questions. It stirs us to look beyond surface answers and instead pursue the depths. When we embrace our doubts with faith, we allow them to teach us, open our eyes to new perspectives, and help us navigate toward our purpose with humility and resilience. Doubt, then, becomes a friend who sharpens our faith and an instructor who gently pushes us toward spiritual maturity.

Consider that each moment of doubt is an opportunity to find the strength within us to move closer to God, to rely on His guidance, and to trust that His purpose for us is as unique as we are. Just as a tree grows stronger by weathering the winds, we, too, grow stronger and more resilient as we lean into our doubts rather than fear them. Through doubt, God invites us to deepen our roots in faith, to branch out beyond what we think we know, and to discover a new resilience.

In embracing doubt, we find that we are part of an unfolding, divine story—a story so vast that it requires each of us to fulfill a unique role. Every question we ask, every doubt we face, weaves us into the fabric of this story, reminding us that we are neither insignificant nor alone. Instead, we are part of God's magnificent plan, each step drawing us nearer to the role only we can play.

So, as we move through life, let us welcome doubt not as a threat but as a guide, a signpost leading us deeper into our purpose and identity. With each question and every hesitation, we are drawn closer to the Creator's vision for us—a purpose so much greater than ourselves. In the end, doubt is not an obstacle but a path to a greater truth, a deeper faith, and a clearer vision of the unique role we are meant to play in this vast, beautiful universe.

Where Doubt Ends, Belonging Begins

At the end of every journey through doubt and questioning, there lies a surprising discovery: a profound sense of belonging. Doubt may have felt like a wilderness, vast and disorienting, but as we navigate it, we find that the path it reveals leads us to something greater—a place where we belong. The questions we've wrestled with and the uncertainties we've confronted all serve to root us more deeply in our true identity and purpose.

Imagine you've journeyed across an expansive landscape, where the horizon always seemed just out of reach, and each step forward revealed new questions. And then, at a certain point, the journey begins to shift. The questions that once unsettled us have led us to a place of peace and clarity as if each step has brought us closer to our unique place in the world. It's here that we find ourselves no longer wandering but arriving—finally stepping into a sense of belonging that feels as though it was waiting for us all along.

In this vast universe, where stars are scattered across endless space, and galaxies swirl in cosmic dances, our place might feel insignificant at first glance. But as we press through our doubts, we begin to see that this grand expanse was designed with intention, with purpose, and that within it, there is a specific place meant for each of us. Doubt was not meant to isolate us; rather, it was a path that led us to understand that we are intricately woven into the fabric of a universe created by a loving God.

When we have faced our doubts and emerged on the other side, we come to see that we are not small or misplaced. We are uniquely positioned in the vastness, each of us holding a purpose that contributes to the greater whole. Like stars in the night sky, each shining with its own light, we find that we belong not in spite of the universe's vastness but because of it. Our questions, our doubts, and our journey through them were never aimless; they were drawing us into this awareness of belonging—a place shaped just for us within God's design.

So, as we let go of doubt, we step into belonging. We realize that every question, every hesitation, and every step of faith has brought us closer to our unique place in this world. And as we stand there, feeling the full weight of our purpose, we understand that we are not only seen but cherished and called. Doubt may have been the journey, but belonging is the destination, a place where we finally feel at home in this vast and marvelous universe.

Chapter 12:

Fragrance Among Thorns — Finding Purpose in Hardship

The idea of this chapter is to explore how, like a rose, our purpose in life can have a subtle but profound impact on others. A rose blooms among thorns, standing out with its vibrant color and gentle fragrance. People may not always see the flower immediately, but the aroma invites them to come closer. The beauty of a rose's fragrance lies not only in its sweetness but also in the reach of its influence. Generally, a rose's scent is most noticeable within a range of 3 to 10 feet—close enough to be experienced by those nearby, yet subtle enough that it's only truly appreciated by those who come close and take notice. In the same way, our purpose, the essence of who we are, often becomes most meaningful and impactful to those around us, even if we are unaware of it.

Beauty Amidst Hardship and Misinterpretation

A rose does not view its thorns as obstacles, nor does it try to remove them. The thorns, though seemingly harsh, are a crucial part of the rose's design, protecting it from predators and enabling it to survive in challenging conditions. Yet, it's easy for us to misinterpret our own thorns—our hardships, perceived flaws, or difficult circumstances—as barriers to our growth. These "false positives" can lead us to think that we're hindered or incomplete. In reality, these thorns often serve a greater purpose, shaping and refining us to bloom fully.

For example, we might view an unexpected setback as a sign of failure, but what if this perceived obstacle is actually preparing us for a greater purpose, like the thorns that protect the rose from harm? These "false positives" can cloud our vision, making us question our place or purpose when, in truth, they're guiding us toward resilience, growth, and eventual beauty.

Strength in Delicacy: Embracing Resilience

The rose's delicate petals are supported by a strong structure, able to endure the heat of the sun, the chill of the night, and even the impact of rain. Similarly, our lives, though often touched by vulnerability, are underpinned by resilience. The "delicate" aspects of our lives—our kindness, empathy, and sensitivity—are not weaknesses; they are strengths that reflect God's grace in us. Misinterpreting these qualities as flaws or liabilities is another false positive. When we see ourselves as "too soft" for a harsh world, we miss the beauty of how our delicacy can uplift others, just as a rose's fragrance and gentle color bring joy.

Rooted in Faith, Guided by Purpose

A rose's roots extend deep into the soil, anchoring it and drawing nourishment, allowing it to bloom regardless of its environment. For us, this soil is our faith. Our roots keep us grounded during the inevitable storms of life, drawing strength from a foundation that is deeper than what the eye can see. During hardship, we might misinterpret these moments of stillness as unproductive—a false positive. Yet, much like the unseen work of roots, these times are essential for us to draw strength, wisdom, and resilience.

In this hidden growth, God prepares us to fulfill our purpose. Often, our most profound growth happens in seasons of waiting and hardship, where our roots of faith are strengthened. What may seem like a lack of progress is actually a period of nourishment, drawing us closer to God and allowing us to bloom in due season.

Purpose Beyond Recognition: The Hidden Fragrance

A rose does not know the effect of its fragrance or see the admiration it inspires. Likewise, our impact on others is often hidden from us. We may underestimate the power of our kindness, the depth of our encouragement, or the joy we bring to those around us. This can lead to another false positive: the belief that, because we don't see the fruit of our efforts, our lives lack meaning or influence. Yet, like the rose's fragrance, our lives carry a purpose that touches others in ways we may never know.

This hidden impact reminds us that our purpose is not self-centered; it is a gift given to us to bless others. The rose's fragrance is for the benefit of all who encounter it, and in the same way, our purpose has an outward impact that often goes beyond what we perceive. We may never know how our lives touch others, but we can trust that God is using us in ways beyond our understanding.

Protection Through Hardship: Finding Purpose in "Thorns"

It's natural to view life's thorns—our struggles, pains, and challenges—as obstacles to avoid. Yet, like the thorns that protect the rose, these hardships often serve to shield us or teach us valuable lessons. The thorns may seem inconvenient or unnecessary, but they guard the rose, keeping it safe from harm. Similarly, what we perceive as "thorns" in our lives might be safeguarding us or leading us to a place of greater purpose.

Sometimes, challenges and obstacles refine our character, teaching us patience, resilience, or compassion. We may not understand their purpose at the moment, but these experiences prepare us for the purpose God has set for us. Recognizing the value of these hardships can transform our perspective, allowing us to see them as integral to our growth rather than obstacles to avoid.

False Positives in Waiting: Misinterpreting the Process

Like the rose, which blooms in its season, we are often called to wait and trust God's timing. However, waiting can be difficult, and it's easy to interpret it as a delay or failure. This is another common false positive—the belief that waiting is wasted time. In reality, waiting is often where God does His most profound work in us, strengthening our character and preparing us for what lies ahead.

Consider the biblical story of David, who was anointed as king but waited years before he took the throne. During this time, he faced trials, developed resilience, and deepened his faith. David's season of waiting was not a failure; it was a period of preparation, allowing him to fulfill his purpose fully when the time came. Like David, we may be in seasons where our purpose is not immediately visible, but these are times to grow deeper in faith and trust.

Purpose Beyond Seasons: Embracing God's Timing

The rose blooms in its season and doesn't rush the process. In the same way, our purpose is revealed in God's timing. There are seasons when we feel hidden, perhaps unnoticed, yet we must trust that God is working in us, preparing us to bloom in the right moment. Just as each rose blooms uniquely, our lives unfold according to God's specific timing and design.

This seasonality reminds us that purpose is not about a final destination or a single achievement. It's a journey, a process of continual growth and blooming at each stage of life. Trusting in God's timing frees us from the anxiety of false positives—the worry that we are not enough or that our lives lack direction. Instead, we can rest in knowing that, just as God cares for the rose, He cares for us, guiding us to our purpose.

Uniqueness and Diversity in Purpose: Celebrating Our Individual "Fragrance"

Roses come in various colors and forms, each with its own beauty and fragrance. Similarly, each of us has a unique purpose, designed to complement rather than compete with others. Comparing ourselves to others is another false positive—an error that leads us to undervalue our unique gifts. Embracing our individuality allows us to contribute our unique fragrance to the world, enriching it in ways that only we can.

Our unique qualities are not flaws; they are intentional designs by God, crafted for His purpose. Just as a garden is made beautiful by diverse flowers, the world is enriched by our unique contributions. When we recognize our own "fragrance" and purpose, we can live authentically, trusting that God has a place for us in His grand design.

Finding Beauty and Purpose Among the Thorns

Our lives, like the rose, are often filled with both beauty and thorns. Each hardship and challenge is an opportunity for growth, shaping us to bloom in God's time. We may not always see our own beauty or impact, but others are blessed by the fragrance of our lives. Through faith, we can embrace our purpose, trusting that each "thorn" is part of God's plan, protecting us, refining us, and allowing us to shine even brighter.

Just as the rose doesn't remove its thorns, we don't need to rid ourselves of every hardship. Instead, we can trust that these thorns serve a purpose, guiding and shaping us to fulfill God's unique design for our lives.

Reflective Questions for Thoughtful Contemplation:

- Are there "thorns" in our lives that we view as obstacles but that might be shaping or protecting us for a greater purpose?

- How can we embrace our own unique "fragrance" or qualities, trusting that they contribute to the world in ways we may not fully see?

- In what ways can we recognize and avoid "false positives," misinterpreting struggles or waiting as failures instead of essential parts of God's plan?

- How might waiting or times of stillness be preparing us for a purpose we cannot yet see?

- Can we, like the rose, trust in God's timing, embracing each season and knowing that we will bloom in His perfect time?

CHAPTER 13:

A JOURNEY OF HEALING – EMBRACING OUR UNIQUE PURPOSE

In this chapter, we explore the story of three blind men whom Jesus healed in different ways, each revealing a profound truth about purpose and God's unique design for each of us. These stories remind us that while we may experience similar struggles, God's approach to our healing, growth, and purpose is as unique as we are. By examining each healing, we see how God's love, timing, and methods reveal the beauty of a purpose that is deeply personal.

The Bold Faith of Bartimaeus: Immediate Healing

Our first story begins with Bartimaeus, whose story is found in Mark 10. He was a blind beggar who called out to Jesus, ignoring the crowd's attempts to silence him. Bartimaeus's healing was immediate—Jesus responded to his boldness and faith without delay. His sight was restored with a single touch, and his life was transformed in that instant. Bartimaeus's faith was assertive and courageous. He didn't hold back but trusted that Jesus would hear him. In his boldness, we see how, sometimes, our purpose is unlocked through an act of faith that overcomes the fear of rejection or the pressure to conform. Bartimaeus teaches us that there are moments when purpose requires us to cry out, take a risk, and approach God with the assurance that He hears and responds.

False Positive Insight: Often, a quick answer or an immediate "yes" can seem to be a mark of true favor, as if faster responses from God are better than waiting. However, Bartimaeus's instant healing isn't a sign that he had more favor than the other two. The timing and method of his healing suited his unique journey and God's purpose for him, not because he was favored over others. This highlights that purpose isn't about how quickly we receive our answers but about what our journey and timing reveal about God's plan.

The Journey of Trust: Gradual Healing of the Man from Bethsaida

In Mark 8, we met another man who was blind. Jesus didn't heal him right away but led him away from the crowd to a private place. There, Jesus applied saliva to his eyes and asked him if he could see. The man's vision was partially restored—he saw people, but they looked like trees walking. Only after a second touch was his sight fully restored. This story illustrates a journey of trust as this man experienced a gradual healing. Unlike Bartimaeus, his purpose wasn't unlocked in an instant but revealed through stages, each one building upon the last. Sometimes, our purpose and healing unfold layer by layer, requiring patience and trust in the process.

False Positive Insight: Many could see a "partial" healing as a sign that his faith was incomplete, or they might question if Jesus's power had somehow faltered. However, the gradual restoration wasn't a flaw in Jesus's power; it was intentional, teaching the man (and us) that sometimes the purpose is revealed progressively. What may appear to us as incomplete or uncertain is actually a step in a broader journey, one that builds trust and dependence on God's timing.

The Path of Obedience: The Healing of the Man Born Blind

Our third story, found in John 9, tells of a man who was born blind. Jesus made mud from His saliva, applied it to the man's eyes, and told him to wash in the Pool of Siloam. Unlike Bartimaeus, who was healed immediately, or the man from Bethsaida, whose healing was gradual, this man's healing required a journey of obedience. He had to take steps in faith, walking to the pool without yet seeing, trusting that healing awaited him. This healing represents the profound purpose found in obedience. The man couldn't yet see, but he acted on Jesus' instructions, embracing a journey without knowing the outcome.

False Positive Insight: To those around him, this man's journey to the pool may have looked pointless or strange—why go through the motions if Jesus could simply heal him on the spot? Yet, this journey was central to his healing, showing us that purpose isn't always direct or instantaneous but sometimes requires steps of faith. The purpose of this man's journey wasn't just physical healing; it was also to cultivate obedience and trust. Sometimes, what seems like a delay or detour is actually God's way of deepening our faith and shaping our character.

Comparing the Three Healings: Unique Paths to Purpose

These three men shared the same condition—blindness—yet each was healed differently. Bartimaeus received his sight immediately, a testament to bold faith. The man from Bethsaida was healed gradually, reflecting a journey of trust. The man born blind was healed through obedience, experiencing a journey with Jesus before the miracle. Their stories reveal that even though their challenges were similar, God's healing approach for each was unique. This diversity in their experiences reminds us that God's purpose is deeply personal.

False Positive Insight: From an outside perspective, people might judge one healing as more "successful" or "miraculous" than another. But God's work in each life was tailored to that individual's heart and journey, revealing that purpose isn't about comparison. Even when two people share similar struggles, God's methods and timing may differ, reflecting a purpose that is personal and specific. Rather than measuring our journey against another's, we're invited to trust that God's work in us is exactly what we need.

The Beauty of the Journey: Walking with Jesus Toward Purpose

For Bartimaeus, the joy of his healing came in the moment, but for the others, it was in the process. The man from Bethsaida and the man born blind walked with Jesus, experienced moments of waiting and trust, and discovered their purpose through the journey itself. The walk with Jesus, the steps taken in faith and trust, were as meaningful as the healing itself. In our own lives, we may find that purpose is not only in the end result but in the journey of walking with Jesus. What if the path of discovery—the waiting, the trust, and the steps of obedience—holds the essence of our purpose?

False Positive Insight: We may sometimes assume that purpose is only in the final healing or completed goal, overlooking the value of the journey itself. However, as these stories reveal, the process of trusting, waiting, and walking in faith with Jesus is often where purpose is forged and understood. Purpose, therefore, is not merely a destination but a journey shaped by God's unique timing and ways.

Embracing Our Own Unique Calling

These three men's stories remind us that purpose is as unique as each individual's journey with God. Though their blindness seemed the same on the surface, the way Jesus healed them differed, tailored to each man's life, heart, and purpose. Likewise, our purpose and healing are designed by God with our specific identity and calling in mind. Just as we cannot compare our journey with others, we cannot compare our purpose. Even if our struggles appear similar, God's approach to our healing and calling is unique. He knows what each of us needs to fulfill our purpose and to grow in our relationship with Him.

In this chapter, may we find peace in our journey, trusting that God's timing, methods, and purpose are exactly what we need. May we embrace our unique calling, knowing that each of us has a distinct role in His kingdom, one that only we can fulfill.

CHAPTER 14:

FEELINGS VS. GOD'S WORD: ANCHORING IN TRUTH BEYOND EMOTION

Feelings are an integral part of the human experience, shaping how we perceive, decide, and interact with the world. They are gifts from God—powerful, vivid, and capable of adding richness to life. Joy, love, hope, and gratitude are beautiful emotions that enhance our experiences. Yet, feelings can also be fleeting and unreliable, clouding judgment and leading us astray if left unchecked. This chapter delves into the nature of feelings, their potential to deceive, and how aligning them with God's Word anchors us in truth, enabling us to live a purposeful and steadfast life.

The Power and Pitfall of Feelings

Feelings can inspire us, motivate action, or serve as warnings, but they can also deceive, confuse, or paralyze us. Take the example of infatuation—it often feels like love but is driven by surface-level attraction or fleeting emotions. Similarly, false peace may arise when we avoid conflict, convincing ourselves that we are "safe," even as unresolved issues grow deeper beneath the surface.

Consider how prideful confidence leads us to overestimate our abilities, relying on ourselves rather than God. Or how guilt can either guide us to repentance or ensnare us in unnecessary shame, overshadowing the truth of God's forgiveness. Subtle feelings like envy, impatience, or fear of missing out (FOMO) tempt us to compare ourselves with others, distracting us from God's unique purpose for our lives.

The deceptive nature of feelings lies in their ability to masquerade as truth. Proverbs 14:12 warns, "There is a way that appears to be right, but in the end, it leads to death." Without discernment, feelings can lure us into decisions that seem right but are far from God's best for us.

Aligning Feelings with God's Word

While feelings are a part of God's design, they are not meant to lead us. God's Word, in contrast, is unchanging, eternal, and wholly reliable. Isaiah 40:8 reminds us, "The grass withers, the flower fades, but the word of our God will stand forever." When emotions shift like sand in the wind, Scripture provides a solid foundation.

Psalm 119:105 says, "Your word is a lamp to my feet and a light to my path." This imagery highlights how Scripture illuminates the steps ahead, guiding us through life's uncertainties. Like a lamp that only brightens the immediate path, God's Word requires us to walk in faith, trusting Him for each step.

Being rooted in Scripture means we must filter our emotions through its truth. When anger rises, James 1:19 reminds us to be "quick to listen, slow to speak, and slow to become angry." When fear threatens, Philippians 4:6-7 encourages us to pray and trust in God's peace. Each verse serves as a compass, steering us toward choices that honor God's will rather than our fleeting emotions.

The False Positives of Feelings

Feelings often create "false positives," convincing us of something untrue. Examples include:

Infatuation masquerading as love: This feeling leads us to form shallow connections without the foundation of commitment and sacrifice.

False peace disguising avoidance: We may feel at ease by ignoring hard truths, but this false peace delays reconciliation and growth.

Envy whispering lies: It tempts us to believe others have better lives, making us overlook God's unique plan for us.

Impatience prompting control: We rush decisions, doubting God's timing, only to realize later the importance of waiting on Him.

These false positives demonstrate why we must regularly test our feelings against Scripture. When emotions arise, ask: "Does this align with God's Word? Does it draw me closer to Him or pull me away?"

God's Word: The Ultimate Anchor

Imagine feelings as waves in a turbulent ocean—sometimes gentle, often overwhelming. Without an anchor, we drift aimlessly, pulled by the current. God's Word is the anchor that keeps us grounded, providing stability and direction.

Consider the parable of the wise and foolish builders in Matthew 7:24-27. The wise man built his house on the rock, symbolizing obedience to God's Word. When storms came, the house stood firm. The foolish man, however, built on shifting sand—his understanding and emotions. When the storms came, his house fell. Where are you building your life?

Practical Examples

Feelings frequently mislead us in relationships. Imagine a scenario where a colleague's tone feels dismissive, leading you to believe they dislike you. Your feelings might drive you to distance yourself, but Proverbs 19:11 reminds us, "A person's wisdom yields patience; it is to one's glory to overlook an offense." By filtering your emotions through Scripture, you choose grace over assumption.

In another example, envy arises when a friend shares their promotion on social media. The feelings of inadequacy and comparison threaten your joy, but Galatians 6:4 advises, "Each one should test their own actions. Then they can take pride in themselves alone, without comparing themselves to someone else." Trusting God's plan for your life frees you from the trap of comparison.

The Journey of Trusting God's Word

Walking by God's Word is a daily discipline. It involves surrendering not just major decisions but every thought and action to His truth. Joshua 1:8 encourages us to "meditate on it day and night." Just as a tree roots itself deeply over time, we must immerse ourselves in Scripture consistently.

Meditating on Scripture transforms our minds, enabling us to discern truth even in emotional storms. When Jesus was tempted in the wilderness, He countered each of Satan's lies with, "It is written…" (Matthew 4:4). This practice equips us to stand firm, responding to deceitful feelings with God's truth.

Creative Reflection: Feelings vs. God's Truth

Picture a traveler navigating a dense forest with a faulty compass that spins erratically. Each step feels uncertain, leading them deeper into confusion. Suddenly, they spot a lighthouse in the distance—steady, unwavering, and guiding them toward safety. God's Word is that lighthouse, cutting through the fog of emotions and providing clarity.

Thoughtful Questions to Reflect On

- When was the last time your feelings led you to a decision you regretted?

- How often do you turn to God's Word for guidance in everyday life?

- Are there specific Scriptures that remind you to trust God's promises over fleeting emotions?

- What steps can you take to make God's Word the foundation of your life?

Anchored in Truth

Feelings are gifts from God, but they are not meant to lead us. Left unchecked, they can deceive and misguide, creating chaos where God intends peace. His Word, however, is steadfast and unchanging, offering clarity, wisdom, and direction in every moment.

To live a life anchored in truth, we must immerse ourselves in Scripture daily. Each verse serves as a guide, helping us navigate emotions with discernment and faith. As we walk with God, each step becomes an act of trust, reflecting His love and wisdom in a world dominated by shifting emotions. Let us choose not the sands of feelings but the unshakable rock of God's Word as the foundation for our lives.

CHAPTER 15:

DISCERNING THE FALSE POSITIVES: SEPARATING TRUTH FROM DECEPTION

False positives are tricky—they often appear as truth, luring us into comfort, safety, or false certainty. In every area of life—relationships, emotions, career decisions, or spiritual beliefs—false positives mislead us into thinking we're on the right path when, in reality, we're deviating from God's truth. This chapter delves deeply into how to identify, navigate, and overcome these deceptive forces by grounding ourselves in God's Word. Through thoughtful reflection, practical tools, and biblical insights, we can discern what is genuine from what is false and live a life aligned with God's purpose.

Understanding False Positives: What Are They?

False positives are deceptive experiences or opportunities that masquerade as truth, goodness, or purpose yet lead us away from what is genuinely fulfilling or aligned with God's plan. Imagine receiving a beautifully wrapped gift only to open it and find it empty—or worse, harmful. That's the essence of false positives: they promise much, but their substance is hollow. These moments appeal to our emotions, desires, or logic yet fail to deliver what they seem to offer, leaving us disillusioned, distracted, or even distant from God. False positives are like mirages in the desert: they shimmer with promise but lead only to emptiness. They appear to satisfy our desires, validate our feelings, or affirm our decisions, but their apparent goodness masks their ultimate futility. These deceptive situations or emotions seem right at the moment but fail to align with God's truth, leaving us further from His purpose for our lives. False positives thrive on human vulnerability, disguising themselves as opportunities, feelings, or solutions that appear ideal but ultimately fall short of God's standard.

The first false positive in history took place in the Garden of Eden. Eve stood before the forbidden tree, listening to the serpent's persuasive words: "You will not surely die… you will be like God, knowing good and evil" (Genesis 3:4-5). The serpent offered what seemed like an extraordinary opportunity—wisdom and power. But it was a twisted version of the truth, enticing Eve to disobey God's direct command. This decision, rooted in the allure of a counterfeit promise, brought sin into the world. The tragedy of this moment wasn't just Eve's disobedience; it was how easily the false positive manipulated her desires, making her believe that what God had already provided wasn't enough.

In today's world, false positives take many forms. Social media, for instance, can create the illusion of connection and validation. A few likes or comments may make us feel seen and valued, but this fleeting affirmation can't replace the deep, authentic relationships God desires for us. Similarly, pursuing wealth might seem like the path to security and happiness, but Scripture warns us that "the love of money is a root of all kinds of evil" (1 Timothy 6:10). Wealth itself isn't wrong, but when it becomes our ultimate goal, it leads us away from trusting in God's provision. Today, false positives are just as pervasive, though they might look different. They thrive in our fast-paced, emotionally charged lives, preying on our insecurities, ambitions, and fears. They come wrapped in feelings of temporary happiness, seemingly ideal opportunities, or advice that sounds wise but subtly deviates from God's Word. For instance, chasing material wealth might feel like achieving success, but it often leaves us spiritually empty. Similarly, entering a relationship based solely on emotional attraction may feel fulfilling at the

104

moment but can lead to heartbreak if the foundation lacks shared faith or values. False positives often hide in the guise of "good things." Consider a career opportunity that offers prestige and financial gain but demands unethical compromises or neglect of family. It looks promising on the surface but pulls us away from the life God has called us to. Even acts of kindness can become false positives if they stem from a desire for recognition rather than genuine love. The danger lies in their subtlety—they rarely scream deception, but whisper promises that align with our wants while diverging from God's truth.

Emotions are a common avenue for false positives. They often feel authentic and powerful but are not always reliable indicators of truth. Think of the fleeting feelings of infatuation that masquerade as love. They can cloud judgment and lead to rushed decisions, like entering a relationship without discernment. Similarly, feelings of false peace might encourage avoidance of conflict or difficult choices, creating a shallow sense of calm that masks deeper issues. Even envy or impatience can disguise themselves as justified reactions, leading us to doubt God's timing or goodness.

False positives also manifest in spiritual contexts, where they are particularly insidious. They might take the form of feel-good theology that prioritizes comfort over conviction, avoiding the harder truths of Scripture in favor of more palatable messages. This creates a false sense of spiritual growth, where we might feel close to God but lack the depth that comes from genuine obedience and sacrifice. For example, rationalizing disobedience by thinking, "God wouldn't ask me to do something so hard," can lead us down a path of convenience rather than true faithfulness.

One of the most dangerous aspects of false positives is their ability to exploit our unmet desires or fears. Consider the fear of being alone, which might drive someone to settle for a relationship that feels "right" but lacks the spiritual alignment necessary for long-term growth. Similarly, the desire for control can lead us to manipulate situations, convincing ourselves we're acting wisely while actually moving away from trusting God's sovereignty.

The story of the Israelites and the golden calf in Exodus 32 is another vivid example of false positives. Frustrated by Moses' delay on Mount Sinai, the people grew impatient and demanded a tangible god to lead them. The golden calf provided an immediate sense of comfort and security but led them into idolatry and away from God's true plan. This illustrates how false positives often exploit our desire for instant gratification, steering us toward what feels accessible or reassuring rather than what is genuinely good.

False positives aren't always dramatic; sometimes, they're subtle shifts in perspective or small compromises that accumulate over time. A busy schedule might feel productive but can become a false positive if it leaves no room for rest or time with God. Pursuing popularity or validation may seem harmless but can distract us from living authentically in Christ. Even well-intentioned advice from friends or mentors can lead us astray if it isn't rooted in Scripture.

These moments are particularly difficult to discern because they align so closely with our human desires. Like counterfeit currency, false positives look convincing but lack the weight and authenticity of the real thing. They appeal to our need for affirmation, purpose, or security but divert us from God's best, offering temporary satisfaction instead of lasting fulfillment.

Recognizing false positives requires self-awareness and a willingness to question what seems obvious. Are we choosing something because it feels right or because it aligns with God's Word? Are we prioritizing short-term comfort over long-term faithfulness? False positives thrive on our tendency to act impulsively, trust our emotions, or follow societal norms without seeking God's perspective.

In essence, false positives are spiritual illusions—shadows of truth that distort our vision and lead us off course. They play on our desire for control, validation, or happiness, promising what only God can truly provide. By understanding their nature, we can begin to see how they operate in our lives and prepare ourselves to navigate them with wisdom and discernment. This understanding is the first step in learning how to separate what is fleeting and deceptive from what is eternal and true.

Recognizing Common False Positives: A Deep Dive

False positives are subtle, often camouflaged within our emotions, desires, or societal norms, and they have the power to lead us astray if not carefully examined. They appear valid, even beneficial, on the surface but fail to align with God's eternal truth. By exploring common false positives in our lives, we can learn to discern between fleeting illusions and God's enduring purpose.

a) Emotions as Certainty

Emotions are a gift from God, designed to enrich our lives, provide signals about our well-being, and deepen our relationships. However, they are also fleeting and subjective, which makes them unreliable as the sole foundation for our decisions. For instance, anger often feels righteous in the heat of the moment, especially when we believe we've been wronged. Yet Proverbs 29:11 warns, "A fool gives full vent to his spirit, but a wise man quietly holds it back." Acting on anger can lead to words we regret, relationships we damage, and decisions that stray from God's will.

Consider the biblical story of Moses striking the rock in anger (Numbers 20:10-11). His frustration with the Israelites led him to

107

disobey God's instructions. While the water still flowed, the act cost Moses his entry into the Promised Land. This false positive—justified anger—appeared reasonable but ultimately disrupted God's plan. Similarly, emotions like envy, resentment, or even fleeting joy can deceive us into thinking a path is right, only to discover it leads us away from God's best.

In everyday life, emotions can mislead us into believing something feels "right" simply because it aligns with our desires. A relationship might feel exciting, but is it grounded in mutual faith and Godly values? A career change might spark enthusiasm, but does it honor God's calling on your life? Evaluating emotions against Scripture helps us navigate these moments with wisdom and clarity.

b) Worldly Success as Fulfillment

In a culture that glorifies achievement, it's easy to equate success with purpose. Society tells us that wealth, accolades, or social status will bring contentment, but Jesus challenges this notion: "What good is it for someone to gain the whole world, yet forfeit their soul?" (Mark 8:36). The pursuit of worldly success often blinds us to the true fulfillment that comes from walking in God's purpose.

Take the parable of the rich fool in Luke 12:16-21. The man hoarded his wealth, building bigger barns to store his surplus, believing he had secured his future. Yet God said to him, "You fool! This very night, your life will be demanded from you." His wealth brought temporary comfort but failed to address his spiritual emptiness. False positives like material wealth or professional accolades can seem like God's blessings, but if they lead us to neglect our relationship with Him, they become distractions rather than gifts.

In practical terms, worldly success might look like securing a prestigious job or building an enviable social media presence. While these accomplishments are not inherently wrong, their value diminishes when they overshadow our eternal purpose. The key question is: Are these successes drawing us closer to God, or are they pulling us away?

c) Fear as a Guide

Fear is one of the most deceptive false positives because it often masquerades as caution, wisdom, or self-preservation. We convince ourselves that avoiding risk or conflict is the safest choice when, in reality, it's a lack of faith in God's provision. 2 Timothy 1:7 reminds us, "For God gave us a spirit not of fear but of power and love and self-control."

The Israelites' journey to the Promised Land provides a stark example. When Moses sent spies to explore Canaan, the majority returned with fearful reports, saying, "We can't attack those people; they are stronger than we are" (Numbers 13:31). Their fear led them to rebel against God, resulting in 40 years of wandering in the wilderness. False positives like fear can seem logical, even protective, but they often prevent us from stepping into God's promises.

In our lives, fear might look like staying in a toxic situation because change feels daunting or avoiding a God-given calling because it seems too big to handle. Instead of letting fear dictate our decisions, we must anchor ourselves in God's Word and trust His guidance, even when the path ahead is uncertain.

d) Misinterpreted Spiritual Signs

In our search for direction, we sometimes rely on "signs" to validate our choices. While God can and does use signs, they must always be evaluated against the unchanging truth of Scripture. Gideon's fleece in Judges 6:36-40 is a famous example of seeking confirmation. Though God honored Gideon's request, this approach reflected Gideon's uncertainty rather than faith. Today, we have the complete Word of God to guide us, reducing the need for external signs.

Misinterpreted signs can lead to significant consequences. A job offer with a higher salary might seem like a "sign" of God's provision, but if it compromises your family time or integrity, it may be a distraction. Similarly, a coincidental encounter might feel like divine affirmation, but without prayerful discernment, it could lead to unwise decisions. Signs can easily align with our desires rather than God's will, making it essential to test them through Scripture and prayer.

e) The Common Thread of False Positives

What makes false positives so dangerous is their subtlety. They often exploit legitimate desires—security, success, love, or direction—and twist them into distractions. These deceptions thrive on half-truths, blending elements of good with underlying motives that pull us away from God. Recognizing them requires humility, vigilance, and a commitment to seeking God's truth above all else.

As believers, we are called to examine everything carefully. 1 Thessalonians 5:21-22 urges us to "test everything; hold fast what is good. Abstain from every form of evil." This means filtering our emotions, opportunities, and decisions through the lens of Scripture, seeking wise counsel, and praying for discernment. False positives will always exist, but by anchoring ourselves in God's Word, we can navigate them with confidence, knowing that His truth will never lead us astray.

The Role of God's Word in Identifying False Positives:

The Bible is our ultimate safeguard against false positives. Hebrews 4:12 declares, "For the word of God is alive and active. Sharper than any double-edged sword, it penetrates even to dividing soul and spirit, joints and marrow; it judges the thoughts and attitudes of the heart." God's Word acts as a filter, helping us distinguish between what is from Him and what is not.

a) Testing Against Scripture

Every decision, feeling, or belief should be tested against the Bible. Ask yourself these guiding questions:

Does this align with God's commandments?

God's laws are timeless truths that safeguard us from harm and lead us toward righteousness. For instance, someone might feel justified in holding onto bitterness because of past hurts. Yet, Scripture says, "Be kind to one another, tenderhearted, forgiving one another, as God in Christ forgave you" (Ephesians 4:32). Any action, thought, or feeling that contradicts His commandments is a clear indicator of a false positive.

Does it glorify God?

Every aspect of our lives should point back to Him. Our ultimate purpose as believers is to glorify God in everything we do (1 Corinthians 10:31). For example, choosing to forgive someone who has wronged us glorifies God by demonstrating His grace and mercy. Even when feelings of resentment feel justified, forgiveness aligns with God's character and brings Him glory. If a decision elevates personal gain, pride, or convenience over glorifying God, it is not from Him.

Does it reflect the character of Christ?

Jesus is the perfect model for living a life that honors God. His life was marked by humility, compassion, obedience, and unwavering faithfulness to God's will. Actions that embody humility, love, and obedience align with His example, while those rooted in selfishness, anger, or pride reveal false positives. For instance, if you're tempted to retaliate against someone who hurt you, remember Jesus' response to His persecutors: "Father, forgive them, for they do not know what they are doing" (Luke 23:34). Choosing to reflect Christ's character, even when it feels counterintuitive, keeps us aligned with God's truth.

b) Seeking Wise Counsel

Proverbs 11:14 reminds us, "Where there is no guidance, a people falls, but in an abundance of counselors, there is safety." Consulting mature Christians who are grounded in Scripture can provide clarity. Wise counsel is invaluable when navigating decisions clouded by emotions or complex circumstances. By inviting trusted believers into our discernment process, we gain perspective and accountability, helping us recognize false positives that may otherwise go unnoticed.

c) Praying for Discernment

James 1:5 promises, "If any of you lacks wisdom, you should ask God, who gives generously to all without finding fault, and it will be given to you." Prayer invites the Holy Spirit to reveal truth and guide us away from deception. Through prayer, we surrender our desires and emotions to God, asking for His wisdom to lead us. This act of humility opens the door for divine guidance, ensuring that our decisions are rooted in His will rather than our own understanding.

Practical Steps to Identify and Avoid False Positives

False positives often disguise themselves as good opportunities, justifiable feelings, or seemingly logical decisions. To avoid being misled, we must approach every situation with intentionality and spiritual discernment. These practical steps provide a roadmap for navigating such challenges with wisdom:

Pause Before Acting

When faced with decisions or emotional situations, it's crucial to pause. False positives thrive on impulsivity, urging us to act quickly without considering the long-term consequences. By pausing, we create space to seek God's guidance and wisdom. Psalm 46:10 reminds us, "Be still, and know that I am God." In moments of stillness, we allow God's voice to cut through the noise of emotions or external pressures. Pausing doesn't mean procrastinating but intentionally slowing down to invite God into the decision-making process.

Consider the example of King Saul in 1 Samuel 13. Facing pressure from the Philistines and his troops, Saul acted impulsively by offering a sacrifice, a role reserved for the prophet Samuel. His failure to pause and wait on God's timing resulted in the loss of his kingdom. This cautionary tale highlights the importance of resisting the urge to act out of fear, impatience, or human reasoning.

Examine Motives

Our motives often reveal the root of our actions. Ask yourself, "Why am I drawn to this choice or feeling? Am I seeking to honor God, or am I prioritizing personal desires, convenience, or approval?" Proverbs 16:2 warns, "All a person's ways seem pure to them, but motives are weighed by the Lord." Even seemingly good actions can stem from impure motives. For example, pursuing a career advancement might appear noble but could be driven by a desire for recognition or material gain rather than glorifying God through work.

In John 6:26, Jesus confronts the crowd following Him after the miracle of feeding the 5,000, saying, "You are looking for me, not because you saw the signs I performed but because you ate the loaves and had your fill." Their motives were rooted in temporary satisfaction rather than a genuine desire for spiritual truth. This challenges us to examine whether our choices align with God's eternal purpose or are influenced by fleeting, self-serving goals.

Track Patterns

Reflecting on past decisions and their outcomes can offer valuable insights. Were there instances where emotions, fear, or worldly values influenced your choices, leading to regret? Identifying these patterns helps us recognize similar scenarios in the future, equipping us to respond with wisdom rather than repetition. Hindsight is a tool for growth, revealing where false positives have previously derailed us.

Think of Peter's denial of Jesus (Luke 22:54-62). Fear and impulsivity led him to deny his Lord three times. However, after reflecting on his failure, Peter became a bold and faithful witness to Christ. His story reminds us that learning from past mistakes can transform us, enabling us to navigate future challenges with greater discernment and faith.

Immerse Yourself in Scripture

Scripture is the ultimate safeguard against false positives. Regular Bible study equips us to distinguish between truth and deception. Psalm 119:11 declares, "I have hidden your word in my heart that I might not sin against you." By deeply embedding God's

Word in our hearts, we create a spiritual lens through which every decision, feeling, and opportunity can be evaluated.

Consider Jesus' response to Satan's temptations in the wilderness (Matthew 4:1-11). Each time, Jesus countered the enemy's lies with the truth of Scripture, saying, "It is written." His example underscores the importance of knowing and applying God's Word when faced with subtle deceptions. Regular engagement with Scripture not only strengthens our faith but sharpens our ability to discern what aligns with God's will.

Rely on the Holy Spirit

The Holy Spirit is our divine guide, providing wisdom and discernment beyond human understanding. John 16:13 promises, "But when he, the Spirit of truth, comes, he will guide you into all the truth." Through prayer and sensitivity to His leading, the Holy Spirit helps us differentiate between fleeting emotions, false positives, and God's enduring truth.

Consider Acts 16:6-10, where Paul and his companions were prevented by the Holy Spirit from entering certain regions. Though they might have perceived their plans as logical and well-intentioned, the Spirit directed them toward Macedonia, where God had a greater purpose for their mission. This illustrates how reliance on the Holy Spirit can redirect us toward God's perfect plan, even when our initial choices seem right.

Biblical Example: David's Decision to Spare Saul

David's encounter with Saul in the cave (1 Samuel 24:1-7) offers a profound lesson on avoiding false positives. The situation seemed perfectly aligned for David to take action. Saul, who had been relentlessly pursuing David to kill him, unknowingly entered the very cave where David and his men were hiding. David's men interpreted the moment as a divine opportunity, saying, "This is the day the Lord spoke of when He said to you, 'I will give your enemy into your hands for you to deal with as you wish.'" To an outsider, it appeared that God had orchestrated Saul's vulnerability to deliver justice into David's hands.

However, David did not let circumstances or the encouragement of his men dictate his actions. Instead, he recognized the danger of a false positive—a situation that seemed right but contradicted God's will. David's response was guided by his deep respect for God's authority. He refrained from harming Saul, saying, "The Lord forbid that I should do such a thing to my master, the Lord's anointed." Despite the compelling circumstances, David understood that seizing the throne through violence would violate God's plan and timing.

This story highlights several key principles for recognizing and avoiding false positives. First, it shows the importance of aligning actions with God's Word, not merely with what seems convenient or logical. David could have justified his actions as self-defense or even divine providence, but he chose to honor God's command not to harm His anointed one. Second, the narrative underscores the value of patience and self-control. David trusted that God's timing was perfect and that acting prematurely would undermine God's greater plan for his life and kingdom.

David's restraint is a reminder that not every open door is from God. What appears to be an opportunity may actually be a test of our character and faith. David chose the harder path—waiting on God—over the seemingly easier path of taking matters into his own hands. His decision demonstrates the importance of seeking God's will in every situation, even when circumstances seem to align with our desires.

Encouragement for the Journey

Recognizing and avoiding false positives is not about achieving perfection but about cultivating discernment through a growing relationship with God. As we immerse ourselves in His Word, seek His guidance in prayer, and rely on the Holy Spirit, we become more attuned to His voice and better equipped to distinguish between what feels right and what truly aligns with His will.

Discerning God's will often involves waiting, as David did, and trusting that His plan is unfolding even when it's not immediately visible. Isaiah 58:11 encourages us: "The Lord will guide you always; He will satisfy your needs in a sun-scorched land and will strengthen your frame." This verse reminds us that God's guidance is constant, and His provision is sufficient, even in difficult seasons.

When faced with situations that seem like divine opportunities, pause and reflect. Ask: Does this align with God's Word? Does it glorify Him? Does it reflect the character of Christ? Just as David demonstrated patience, humility, and faithfulness in the cave, we are called to approach every decision with these qualities, trusting that God's ways are higher than ours.

Ultimately, avoiding false positives is about surrendering control to God and allowing His truth to shape our responses. The journey may be challenging, but it is also deeply rewarding. By walking in obedience, we experience the peace and purpose that come from living in alignment with God's will. Let David's story serve as a beacon, reminding us that true victory lies not in taking matters into our own hands but in trusting the One who holds all things in His hands.

CHAPTER 16:

BECOMING GOD'S PERFECT VERSION

As a software system engineer, I often encounter the critical importance of compatibility. Imagine working on a project where you're using Python 3, but you accidentally install a version of pip that's incompatible. The result? Frustration, inefficiency, and a barrage of errors that halt progress. This real-world example resonates deeply with our spiritual lives. Just as software versions must align for systems to function properly, our lives must align with God's design to flourish. This chapter explores how becoming God's perfect version of ourselves requires intentionality, surrender, and transformation.

The Importance of Alignment

In software, a mismatch between versions creates dysfunction and delays. Similarly, when we try to live outside God's plan, we experience spiritual errors: confusion, frustration, and a sense of emptiness. God has uniquely designed each of us with a specific purpose, a unique "version" of who we are meant to be. However, how often do we find ourselves running on "self-upgraded" versions dictated by societal pressures, personal desires, or misguided expectations? Proverbs 3:5-6 encourages us to "Trust in the Lord with all your heart and lean not on your own understanding; in all your ways submit to Him, and He will make your paths straight." Trusting God means accepting His updates to our lives and knowing that His design is not just better but perfect.

Version Updates and Transformation

As a system evolves, software requires updates to remain secure, efficient, and relevant. Similarly, our spiritual growth requires regular updates to align more closely with God's purpose. Romans 12:2 reminds us, "Do not conform to the pattern of this world, but be transformed by the renewing of your mind." Transformation is a continuous process, akin to updating our spiritual "operating system" to keep it running smoothly under God's guidance.

Resisting updates in software eventually leads to vulnerabilities, inefficiencies, and breakdowns. Likewise, when we resist God's call to grow or change, we become spiritually stagnant, vulnerable to temptation, and disconnected from our purpose. Embracing His transformation allows us to leave behind outdated habits, thoughts, and behaviors, enabling us to function as He intended.

The Pitfall of Compatibility Issues

Incompatibility in software is frustrating—it wastes time and compromises productivity. In our lives, similar mismatches occur when our values, actions, or desires are not aligned with God's truth. For instance, pursuing worldly success might seem like a blessing, but if it leads us to neglect family, faith, or integrity, it becomes a false positive—a path that looks promising but pulls us away from God.

Jesus emphasizes this in Matthew 6:24: "No one can serve two masters. Either you will hate the one and love the other, or you will be devoted to the one and despise the other." This incompatibility between worldly pursuits and godly living underscores the importance of aligning every aspect of our lives with His purpose.

God's Perfect Version Is Unique

Each software has a distinct version tailored for specific environments and tasks. Similarly, God's version of you is uniquely designed. Psalm 139:14 declares, "I praise you because I am fearfully and wonderfully made." Becoming God's version of yourself doesn't mean conforming to a worldly mold but stepping into the unique identity He has crafted for you. To achieve this, we must uninstall the "programs" of comparison, pride, and self-reliance and install faith, humility, and dependence on Him.

Debugging Life's Errors

When software encounters bugs, developers debug the code to identify and fix the issues. Similarly, when our lives encounter problems, it's often a sign of misalignment with God's will. These "bugs" could be toxic relationships, unwise decisions, or spiritual complacency. Debugging our lives involves prayer, reflection, and seeking God's guidance to identify root causes and implement His solutions. James 1:5 encourages us, "If any of you lacks wisdom, you should ask God, who gives generously to all without finding fault, and it will be given to you." God, as the ultimate debugger, offers clarity, healing, and restoration when we turn to Him.

Practical Lessons from Software Systems

Consistent Updates: Like regularly updating software, we must consistently immerse ourselves in Scripture and prayer to stay aligned with God.

Error Logs: Reflect on past mistakes and patterns to understand areas needing correction.

Testing and Debugging: Test every decision against God's Word, seeking wise counsel and relying on the Holy Spirit for discernment.

Final Reflection

God's version of you is not about conforming to a worldly ideal or striving to meet fleeting standards of success or approval; it's about becoming the person He envisioned when He created you. You are made in His image (Genesis 1:27), reflecting His character, love, and creativity. God's ultimate purpose for your life is to draw closer to Him daily, becoming more like Christ and living a life that glorifies Him.

Every day is an opportunity to grow closer to God and to align your thoughts, actions, and desires with His heart. This journey is not about perfection but about progress—allowing God to shape you through His Word, His Spirit, and His plans. As you walk with Him, remember that your purpose is not just about what you do but who you are in Him. You are the light of the world, called to shine brightly in the darkness (Matthew 5:14). You are the salt of the earth, bringing flavor, preservation, and value to a world in need (Matthew 5:13). You are a city on a hill, unhidden and radiant, showcasing God's glory to all who see (Matthew 5:14-16).

You are not a mistake or an afterthought. You are fearfully and wonderfully made, designed with intention and love by the Creator of the universe (Psalm 139:14). Your unique gifts, experiences, and even your struggles are part of the tapestry God is weaving for His glory and your good. He does not want you to blend into the patterns of this world but to stand out as His masterpiece (Ephesians 2:10).

Living as God's version of yourself means embracing your role as His image-bearer and reflecting His light in everything you do. It means seeking to glorify Jesus in your relationships, your work, your choices, and even your dreams. It means understanding that your purpose isn't about comparison or competition but about fulfilling the unique calling God has placed on your life.

God sees you as special and irreplaceable. Just as no two fingerprints are alike, no two callings are identical. Your journey is yours alone, and it is divinely designed to bring you closer to Him while revealing His love to the world. When you live in alignment with God's plan, you experience the peace, joy, and fulfillment that only He can provide.

Allow God to be your divine developer, the One who refines you, corrects you, and calls you to a higher version of yourself—His version. Trust in His timing, surrender to His will, and walk boldly in the identity He has given you. As Philippians 1:6 reminds us, "He who began a good work in you will carry it on to completion until the day of Christ Jesus."

Let your life be a reflection of His image, a beacon of hope, and a testimony of His grace. You are chosen, cherished, and commissioned to live for His glory. Embrace this truth and step forward with confidence, knowing that every day brings you closer to becoming God's perfect version of yourself.

CHAPTER 17:

THE SHORTEST PATH ALGORITHM: PRIORITIZING YOUR STEPS TOWARD PURPOSE

In the real world, algorithms like the shortest path algorithm are essential for solving complex problems efficiently. From determining optimal flight paths to navigation systems, this algorithm identifies the quickest way to get from point A to point C by minimizing time, distance, or effort. But what happens when we apply this concept to our spiritual lives? Let's explore how the principles of the shortest path algorithm can offer profound insights into prioritizing our steps toward fulfilling our God-given purpose.

The Real-World Analogy: Choosing the Direct Route

Imagine you're navigating through three nodes: A, B, and C. Let A represent yourself, B represent Jesus, and C represent someone significant in your life—perhaps your boss, a family member, or an influential figure. In practical terms, the shortest path between A and C would naturally be a direct connection. It seems logical: go straight to C, avoid unnecessary steps, and achieve your goal faster.

But in the spiritual world, the path that appears shortest isn't always the most effective or meaningful. Instead, the path from A to B to C—where you prioritize connecting with Jesus first—leads to greater fulfillment, clarity, and purpose. Why? Because when you focus on Jesus, you allow Him to guide, influence, and even soften the hearts of those you wish to reach.

The Spiritual Reality: Seeking God First

Proverbs 21:1 reminds us, "The king's heart is in the hand of the Lord; He directs it like a watercourse wherever He pleases." This verse highlights a profound truth: God holds ultimate authority over every person and situation. When you approach Jesus first (A → B), you align yourself with His will, allowing Him to direct the path to others (B → C).

However, as humans with fleshly tendencies, we often attempt to bypass Jesus and go straight to people or situations we want to influence. This leads to exhaustion, frustration, and feelings of inadequacy. We forget that it's not our job to change hearts—it's God's. By seeking Jesus first, we invite Him to work on our behalf, clearing the path to our destination and ensuring that our steps glorify Him.

Biblical Foundation: The Kingdom's First Principle

Matthew 6:33 provides the perfect foundation for this concept: "But seek first His kingdom and His righteousness, and all these things will be given to you as well." When we prioritize God in our decisions and actions, we shift our focus from human approval to divine alignment. The result? We achieve not only our goals but also the deeper purpose of glorifying God through our lives.

The Illusion of the "Direct" Path

On the surface, choosing the direct path from A (yourself) to C (a person or goal) seems efficient and logical. It avoids detours, saves time, and aligns with how we're wired to seek quick results. Yet, this seemingly straightforward route often leads to disappointment and frustration, especially in the spiritual realm. Let's delve deeper into why bypassing Jesus (B) in the journey creates more challenges than solutions.

1. Misplaced Effort: The Heavy Burden of Pleasing Others

When we attempt to go directly to people or situations, we rely entirely on our own abilities to make things work. This often means bending over backward to gain approval, meet expectations, or achieve a particular outcome. While it may seem achievable at first, the effort quickly becomes exhausting. Why? Because human approval is fickle, and the goalposts constantly shift.

For example, you might go out of your way to please a boss, a friend, or even a family member, only to feel undervalued or ignored. The harder you try, the more it feels like your efforts are not enough. This misplaced effort becomes a heavy burden because it's rooted in the need for validation from people rather than the unchanging approval of God.

When we start with Jesus, however, we gain perspective. Colossians 3:23 reminds us, "Whatever you do, work at it with all your heart, as working for the Lord, not for human masters." Starting with Him lightens the burden, as we're no longer driven by the need to please others but by the assurance that God already accepts us.

2. Unpredictable Outcomes: The Risk of Human Reactions

People are unpredictable. Their responses are influenced by countless factors—mood, circumstances, biases, or even misunderstandings. When we approach people directly, expecting a specific outcome, we set ourselves up for potential disappointment.

Imagine pouring your heart into a project at work, hoping for recognition, only to be met with indifference. Or consider seeking affirmation from a friend who is too preoccupied with their struggles to notice your efforts. These moments sting because they highlight the uncertainty of relying solely on human reactions.

By going to Jesus first, we entrust these situations to the One who understands every heart and can turn circumstances in our favor. Proverbs 21:1 reassures us, "The king's heart is in the hand of the Lord; He directs it like a watercourse wherever He pleases." While people may be unpredictable, God's sovereignty remains constant. He can influence hearts and situations in ways we never could on our own.

3. Spiritual Emptiness: The Cost of Bypassing Jesus

When we bypass Jesus and focus solely on human approval or worldly goals, we miss out on His peace, wisdom, and provision. This creates a spiritual void that leaves us feeling drained and unfulfilled, even if we achieve what we initially set out to do.

Consider this: you secure a promotion or repair a strained relationship without seeking Jesus. On the surface, it feels like a victory, but there's an underlying emptiness because the process lacked His presence and guidance. Achievements and relationships, when pursued without God, often fail to bring lasting joy or peace.

Jesus invites us to lay our burdens at His feet, promising rest and renewal. In Matthew 11:28-30, He says, "Come to me, all you who are weary and burdened, and I will give you rest. Take my yoke upon you and learn from me, for I am gentle and humble in heart, and you will find rest for your souls." When we start with Jesus, we're filled with His peace, regardless of the outcome. This spiritual fulfillment cannot be replicated by worldly successes or human validation.

In contrast, taking the path through Jesus (A → B → C) brings assurance that your steps are in line with His will. Even if the journey feels longer, it's marked by His presence, power, and purpose.

Jesus: The Ultimate Mediator

The Bible describes Jesus as our mediator (1 Timothy 2:5), bridging the gap between humanity and God. Just as He intercedes for us before the Father, Jesus also works in our relationships and endeavors. When you seek Him first, you entrust your goals and interactions to the One who knows the end from the beginning.

An Encouraging Example: Nehemiah's Prayerful Approach

Nehemiah's story in the Bible offers a powerful illustration of this principle. When Nehemiah learned of Jerusalem's ruined walls, he didn't rush to the king (C) for permission to rebuild. Instead, he first sought God (B) through prayer and fasting (Nehemiah 1:4-11). By the time he approached the king, God had already prepared the king's heart to grant Nehemiah favor (Nehemiah 2:8). This demonstrates the beauty of going through Jesus: He works behind the scenes, ensuring that even human authority aligns with His divine plan.

Final Reflection: Trusting the Longer, Better Path

The shortest path algorithm in the spiritual world teaches us a profound truth: the most effective and fulfilling journey is not always the quickest one. While it may seem logical to go directly to people or situations to seek approval, resolve conflicts, or achieve goals, the true path begins with Jesus. He is the source of wisdom, the One who directs hearts, and the only One capable of aligning our steps with God's ultimate purpose for our lives.

Choosing the path that starts with Jesus (A → B → C) often requires patience, trust, and surrender. It may feel counterintuitive, especially when the world urges us to chase immediate solutions or validation. But this path is the one where transformation happens.

It's where God refines us, reveals His plans, and ensures that our efforts are rooted in His truth. It's also the path that protects us from the deception of false positives—those alluring shortcuts that seem right but ultimately lead us astray.

The Better Path: Aligning with God's Purpose

The longer path through Jesus ensures that our lives align with His will. When we begin with Him, we allow His Word and presence to filter our decisions, removing the noise of fleeting emotions, societal pressures, and personal fears. Jesus becomes the lens through which we view every relationship, opportunity, and challenge.

Proverbs 3:5-6 reminds us, "Trust in the Lord with all your heart and lean not on your own understanding; in all your ways submit to Him, and He will make your paths straight." Submitting to God's plan means accepting that His ways are higher and better than our own. It means trusting that He knows the end from the beginning and that His timing is perfect.

A Path Free from False Positives

Starting with Path B—Jesus also protects us from false positives—those deceptive paths that seem right but lead to regret. When we seek validation, solutions, or direction without consulting Him, we risk making decisions based on incomplete understanding or fleeting emotions. However, when we go to Path B—Jesus first, we ensure that our choices are grounded in His unchanging truth and His divine wisdom.

For example, pursuing a career opportunity without prayer and discernment might lead to temporary success but spiritual emptiness. Similarly, seeking approval from others (Path C) without first seeking approval from Jesus (Path B) can leave us feeling undervalued, insecure, and constantly chasing validation. Path B—Jesus redirects our focus toward God's perfect plan, anchoring our decisions in His promises and aligning us with His will.

By starting with Jesus, we avoid the pitfalls of worldly shortcuts and find clarity, peace, and purpose in His guidance. It reminds us that seeking Him first is not just the better path—it's the only path that leads to a life rooted in truth and eternal significance.

The Purpose Beyond the Path

Our purpose is not to please people or achieve worldly success—it is to glorify God. As we walk with Jesus, we become a reflection of His love, grace, and truth. This is why the path that starts with Him is not only better but also transformational. It shapes us into His likeness, aligning our lives with His mission to bring light to the world.

In Matthew 5:14-16, Jesus declares, "You are the light of the world. A town built on a hill cannot be hidden. Neither do people light a lamp and put it under a bowl. Instead, they put it on its stand, and it gives light to everyone in the house. In the same way, let your light shine before others, that they may see your good deeds and glorify your Father in heaven." When we start with Jesus, our journey becomes a testimony of His faithfulness and goodness, drawing others to Him.

A Daily Commitment

Walking the longer, better path isn't a one-time decision—it's a daily commitment. Each day presents opportunities to choose between the world's shortcuts and God's way. Will we seek immediate gratification, or will we trust in God's process? Will we rely on our understanding, or will we surrender to His wisdom?

As we anchor ourselves in Jesus, we find clarity in our purpose. Every step, no matter how small, becomes a meaningful part of the journey He has planned for us. The longer path is not just about reaching a destination—it's about growing in faith, character, and intimacy with God along the way.

An Invitation to Trust

The path through Jesus may not always feel easy, but it is the path of assurance, peace, and eternal significance. He invites us to trust Him with every decision, every relationship, and every challenge. As Isaiah 30:21 says, "Whether you turn to the right or the left, your ears will hear a voice behind you, saying, 'This is the way; walk in it.'" His voice guides us, His love sustains us, and His plans never fail.

So, as you navigate your journey, remember this: Your purpose is not defined by worldly achievements but by your relationship with Jesus. You are called to glorify Him, to trust Him, and to reflect His light in all you do. Let Him be your starting point, your guide, and your destination. By choosing the longer, better path through Jesus, you will not only fulfill your purpose but also experience the joy and peace of walking in step with God's perfect will.

CHAPTER 18:

JESUS: THE DIVINE SERVER OF CONNECTION AND CLARITY

In our increasingly digital world, we rely on networks and servers to stay connected. From video calls to instant messaging, the quality of these connections often determines the success of our communication. But what happens when the server fails? Messages lag, calls drop, and frustration builds. Thankfully, our spiritual connection through Jesus is entirely different. Jesus is the ultimate "server"—unfailing, omnipresent, and always available. In this chapter, we explore how Jesus ensures an unbroken, direct connection between us and the Father, offering clarity, purpose, and peace.

The End-to-End Connection

In a typical communication network, data is sent from one point to another. Often, a third-party server mediates this process, potentially introducing delays, errors, or even breaches of trust. However, Jesus eliminates the need for intermediaries. Through Him, we have direct access to God. John 14:6 reminds us of this truth: "I am the way and the truth and the life. No one comes to the Father except through me."

This end-to-end connection means that every prayer, every cry, and every thought directed toward God passes through Jesus with perfect clarity. There are no miscommunications, no delays, and no distortions. Unlike earthly servers, which require updates and maintenance, Jesus is unchanging and eternal, ensuring that our connection remains steadfast.

No Missed Calls in His Chatbox

Imagine messaging a friend in distress, only to be left on "read." In our human relationships, missed calls and unanswered texts can leave us feeling isolated and undervalued. But Jesus' chat box is different. Jeremiah 33:3 assures us, "Call to me, and I will answer you and tell you great and unsearchable things you do not know." When we reach out to Him, He always responds, even when His answer isn't immediate or in the form we expect.

Unlike human connections that depend on schedules, mood, or availability, Jesus is available 24/7. His chat box has no backlog of unread messages, no delays in responses, and no system crashes. Every message sent to Him is received with undivided attention and answered with perfect wisdom.

A Network Without Errors

In earthly communication systems, network errors are common. Weak signals, incompatible software, and server overloads can disrupt the flow of information. But in our spiritual communication, Jesus ensures a flawless network. Ephesians 2:18 says, "For through Him we both have access to the Father by one Spirit."

Jesus acts as the divine server that processes our prayers, intentions, and desires, ensuring they reach the Father in their purest form. Even when our prayers are clumsy or unclear, the Holy Spirit intercedes, translating our groans into words that align with God's will (Romans 8:26-27). This divine network has no server downtime, no interruptions, and no compatibility issues.

No Weak Internet Connection

In the digital world, a weak internet connection can render even the most advanced technology useless. Similarly, in our spiritual lives, distractions, doubt, and sin can weaken our sense of connection to God. However, Jesus strengthens and sustains our connection, ensuring that no interference can sever our relationship with Him. Romans 8:38-39 declares, "For I am convinced that neither death nor life, neither angels nor demons, neither the present nor the future, nor any powers... will be able to separate us from the love of God that is in Christ Jesus our Lord."

When we prioritize Jesus as our server, our spiritual "signal" remains strong, even in the face of life's challenges. Whether we are in a season of joy or struggle, our connection to Him is unwavering.

Reliable and Secure Communication

In earthly systems, data breaches and privacy concerns are common. But with Jesus, our communication is completely secure. Hebrews 4:16 invites us to "approach God's throne of grace with confidence." We can share our deepest fears, desires, and confessions, knowing that our communication with Him is confidential and protected.

Unlike human networks that store and exploit data, Jesus' network is built on love and grace. He listens without judgment, responds with compassion, and provides guidance tailored specifically to our needs.

Seeking and Finding in His Network

One of the most profound aspects of Jesus as our server is the promise that seeking Him always leads to discovery. Matthew 7:7-8 says, "Ask, and it will be given to you; seek, and you will find; knock, and the door will be opened to you." In this divine network, no message goes unanswered, no search returns empty, and no effort to connect is wasted.

Jesus ensures that our seeking leads to clarity. Whether we're seeking direction in life, understanding Scripture, or comfort in difficult times, He provides answers that are timely and true. His responses are not automated or generic but deeply personal, reflecting His intimate knowledge of our hearts.

The Purpose of the Divine Network

Why does Jesus act as our server, ensuring this flawless connection? The answer lies in His love for us and His desire for us to fulfill our God-given purpose. Just as a server facilitates communication between users, Jesus bridges the gap between humanity and God, empowering us to live lives that glorify Him.

When we rely on Jesus for guidance, we align our steps with God's perfect plan. This alignment helps us avoid false positives—those deceptive paths that seem right but lead to regret. By prioritizing our connection with Him, we ensure that our decisions, relationships, and actions are rooted in truth.

Final Reflection: Stay Connected

The divine network through Jesus stands unparalleled—it is reliable, secure, and unwavering in its availability. Unlike any earthly system, it functions without interruptions, miscommunication, or errors. This network is a lifeline connecting us directly to the Father, ensuring that every prayer, every cry, and every thought is heard and answered according to His perfect will. His network never goes down, His responses are never delayed, and His guidance is always precise.

Staying connected to Jesus isn't a passive experience; it's an active commitment. It involves seeking Him intentionally, trusting Him wholeheartedly, and aligning every aspect of your life with His Word. When you place Jesus at the center of your decisions, relationships, and goals, you can avoid the false positives that so often lead us astray. False positives—those deceptive paths, feelings, or opportunities that seem right but ultimately lead to regret—are filtered out when you rely on His perfect network of grace and truth.

Consider the example of decision-making. When faced with a difficult choice, the world might offer many "direct paths" that seem quick and logical. However, these shortcuts often ignore God's will, leading to confusion, disappointment, or missed blessings. By staying connected to Jesus and seeking His guidance first, you ensure that your steps are aligned with His purpose. Proverbs 3:5-6 reminds us to "trust in the Lord with all your heart and lean not on your own understanding; in all your ways submit to Him, and He will make your paths straight."

Avoiding False Positives Through Connection

The divine network through Jesus is not just a source of comfort; it is a safeguard against deception. When you stay connected to Him, He provides clarity that cuts through the noise of emotions, worldly distractions, and external pressures. False positives thrive in confusion, but Jesus illuminates the truth with His unchanging Word. His guidance ensures that your decisions are not driven by fleeting feelings, fear, or societal expectations but by eternal principles.

For instance, feelings of inadequacy might tempt you to seek validation from others, but staying connected to Jesus reminds you that your worth comes from being a child of God (Ephesians 2:10). Similarly, the allure of worldly success might push you toward decisions that prioritize ambition over faith, but His Word redirects you to seek first His kingdom and righteousness (Matthew 6:33).

A Network Built on Trust and Faith

Unlike human networks that require constant upgrades, Jesus' network is already perfect. However, our connection requires maintenance through faith, prayer, and Scripture. Each day presents an opportunity to deepen your connection and ensure that you're walking in His will. By anchoring your life in His truth, you build resilience against the doubts and temptations that can sever your spiritual connection.

This connection also strengthens your discernment. The more you rely on Jesus, the more clearly you'll recognize false positives for what they are—distractions that pull you away from God's best. His Word becomes a filter, helping you evaluate every opportunity, decision, or relationship with clarity and wisdom. As Psalm 119:105 says, "Your word is a lamp to my feet and a light to my path."

Walking in Peace and Purpose

When you are actively connected to Jesus, you experience a profound sense of peace and purpose. This peace doesn't come from circumstances but from the assurance that you are walking in alignment with God's plan. His network doesn't just connect you to Him; it also aligns you with the people, opportunities, and paths that fulfill your divine purpose.

Through this connection, you gain a deeper understanding of who you are in Christ. You are the light of the world (Matthew 5:14), a vessel of His love and truth. Your purpose becomes clear—not to seek validation from the world but to glorify God in all that you do. And as you walk in obedience, you become a beacon of hope, pointing others toward the same unshakable connection.

An Unfailing Network for Every Season

Life is full of challenges, uncertainties, and moments of doubt. Yet, Jesus' network remains constant through every season. Whether you're in a period of waiting, decision-making, or growth, His connection never wavers. By staying connected, you tap into a source of strength, wisdom, and guidance that transcends human limitations.

This divine network isn't just for the big moments; it's for the everyday steps that make up your journey. When you wake up anxious, His Word reminds you to cast your cares on Him (1 Peter 5:7). When you feel overwhelmed, His Spirit whispers peace that surpasses understanding (Philippians 4:7). Every moment becomes an opportunity to rely on Him, ensuring that your life reflects His purpose and glory.

The Call to Stay Connected

The invitation to stay connected to Jesus is not a one-time call but a daily commitment. It's about choosing Him first in every situation, seeking His guidance before acting, and trusting His plan even when it's not immediately clear. In doing so, you avoid the pitfalls of false positives and walk confidently in the path He has set before you.

As you navigate the complexities of life, remember that Jesus is your divine server, your ultimate connection to truth, peace, and purpose. In Him, there are no missed calls, no unanswered prayers, and no failed connections. Trust Him, seek Him, and allow His unchanging love to guide every step of your journey. By staying connected, you'll discover the fullness of life that only He can provide—free from deception, filled with purpose, and anchored in eternal truth.

CHAPTER 19:

STONES IN THE RIVER: REMAINING UNSHAKEN IN A WORLD OF FALSE POSITIVES

In the midst of rushing waters, a stone remains steadfast, unyielding to the currents around it. Even after years of being submerged in the river, its core remains untouched by the water. This remarkable characteristic offers a profound lesson for our spiritual lives: while we live in a world filled with pressures, distractions, and false positives, we are called to remain grounded and impervious to the forces that seek to infiltrate our hearts and minds.

The Stone and the River: A Metaphor for Resilience

Picture a stone lying at the bottom of a river. It is surrounded by water and the current flows constantly against it. Yet, no matter how long it remains submerged, the stone does not absorb the water. Its surface may smoothen over time, its edges shaped by the flow, but its core stays intact. This unwavering resistance reminds us that, as believers, we are to be in the world but not of it.

Even if one were to later take the stone and break it open, the inside would remain dry—completely untouched by the water that surrounded it for so long. This detail emphasizes the depth of the stone's resilience, a metaphor for how we must guard our inner lives from worldly influences. Similarly, our hearts, when protected by God's Word and filled with His Spirit, remain untouched by the distractions and false promises of the world around us.

Jesus prayed for us in John 17:15-16, saying, "My prayer is not that you take them out of the world but that you protect them from the evil one. They are not of the world, even as I am not of it." The stone's resilience against the water illustrates how we, too, can resist the false positives and temptations that surround us daily.

The Pressure of the Current

The river's current represents the constant flow of worldly influences—pressures to conform, to compromise, or to chase fleeting pleasures. These influences are relentless, much like the water pushing against the stone. Yet, the stone doesn't fight the current; it simply stands firm.

In our lives, the "current" might take the form of societal expectations, the allure of material success, or the fear of missing out. It could be the pressure to blend in with the crowd or to follow trends that contradict God's Word. These false positives, though appealing on the surface, lead us away from our purpose. Romans 12:2 reminds us, "Do not conform to the pattern of this world, but be transformed by the renewing of your mind." Like the stone, we are called to remain steadfast, trusting in God's truth rather than being swept away by the currents around us.

Remaining Impervious to False Positives

The stone's ability to resist water infiltration is a reminder that we, too, have the capacity to guard our hearts and minds. Proverbs 4:23 says, "Above all else, guard your heart, for everything you do flows from it." Guarding our hearts means being vigilant about what we allow to influence us—whether it's through media, relationships, or our own thoughts.

False positives often appear subtle. They might come as opportunities that seem too good to be true or emotions that feel justified in the moment. However, by remaining anchored in God's Word, we can discern truth from deception. Like the stone that refuses to let water penetrate its core, we can choose to stand firm against these distractions, rooted in faith and trust in God.

Shaped but Not Broken

Over time, the river smoothens the stone, refining its surface through constant contact with water and sediment. While the stone remains steadfast, its rough edges are gradually worn away, leaving behind a polished exterior. This natural process mirrors the spiritual journey of our lives—where trials and challenges refine us, shaping us into the individuals God designed us to be.

James 1:2-4 encourages us to embrace this process, saying, "Consider it pure joy, my brothers and sisters, whenever you face trials of many kinds, because you know that the testing of your faith produces perseverance. Let perseverance finish its work so that you may be mature and complete, not lacking anything." Trials, while uncomfortable and sometimes overwhelming, are not meant to break us but to strengthen and purify us. They serve as divine tools, chiseling away our imperfections and preparing us to reflect God's glory more fully.

The river's current is relentless, yet it does not destroy the stone. Similarly, the pressures we face in life—whether through personal loss, relational struggles, or professional challenges—may feel unyielding, but they are part of God's intentional design to refine us. These moments teach us patience as we wait for God's timing, humility as we recognize our dependence on Him, and trust as we learn to let go of our own understanding and lean into His wisdom.

Yet, amidst this refinement, the core of the stone remains untouched. This is a profound reminder that when our lives are anchored in Christ, the essence of who we are—our identity as

God's beloved children—remains protected. The trials may shape us externally, but they cannot infiltrate or damage the foundation of our faith. Psalm 62:6 declares, "Truly He is my rock and my salvation; He is my fortress, I will not be shaken." This unshakable core is a testament to the power of God's grace and protection.

The refining process is not always easy. It can feel like we're being chipped away or submerged under the weight of life's demands. However, just as the stone emerges more beautiful and resilient after years in the river, we, too, emerge stronger and more aligned with God's purpose. Each challenge we face is an opportunity for growth, a chance to become more like Christ.

Consider how a river-polished stone is often used for a specific purpose—whether as a building block, a decorative piece, or a tool. In the same way, God refines us not only for our benefit but for His greater plan. He shapes us so that we can be instruments of His love, vessels of His truth, and reflections of His character to the world.

The process of being shaped but not broken also reminds us of our role in the community. Just as stones in a river may smooth each other through contact, our relationships and interactions with others can refine us. Sometimes, the challenges we face are rooted in these connections, yet they are opportunities for growth in love, patience, and forgiveness. Proverbs 27:17 says, "As iron sharpens iron, so one person sharpens another." The friction we experience with others, guided by God's hand, can lead to mutual refinement and spiritual maturity.

Lessons from the Stone

The stone in the river teaches us several key lessons:

Stand Firm in Faith: Just as the stone withstands the current, we must hold fast to God's Word and not be swayed by worldly influences.

Guard Your Heart: Like the stone's impermeable core, we must protect our hearts from false positives, ensuring that our decisions and actions align with God's truth.

Embrace Refinement: Allow God to shape you through life's challenges, trusting that He is preparing you for His purpose.

Be a Beacon of Strength: The stone's steadfastness in the river is a testament to its resilience. Similarly, your unwavering faith can inspire and encourage others to stand firm in their walk with Christ.

Final Reflection: Living Like the Stone

In this world, it's easy to feel overwhelmed by the currents of life. The pressures to conform, the allure of false positives, and the trials we face can all seem relentless. However, like the stone in the river, we are called to remain steadfast, anchored in God's truth.

Even when life breaks us open, like the stone shattered after years in the river, let it be revealed that our core remains untouched—protected by the grace of God and impervious to the falsehoods of the world. This unshakable resilience is a testimony to the power of faith and trust in Jesus.

Every day, choose to let God's Word be your foundation. Seek Him first, trusting that His plans for you are good and perfect. Remember, your purpose is not to blend into the current but to stand out as a testimony of God's grace and strength.

Just as the stone resists the water, let us resist the false positives that seek to infiltrate our lives. Let us be shaped by God's hands, not broken by the world. And as we live out our faith, may our

142

steadfastness inspire others to anchor themselves in Christ, the source of true purpose and peace.

CHAPTER 20:

RECOGNIZING GOD'S VOICE: THE DIVINE CALL IN A NOISY WORLD

Recognizing God's voice is not merely a skill; it is the foundation of a thriving relationship with Him. In the cacophony of life, filled with competing demands, fleeting emotions, and endless opinions, His voice is the compass that provides direction, clarity, and assurance. This chapter explores the significance of hearing God's voice, the challenges that obscure it, and the profound transformation it brings when we tune our spiritual ears to Him.

Why Recognizing God's Voice Matters

God's voice is not just guidance—it is the lifeline to our identity and purpose. Hearing Him transforms every moment of our lives, enabling us to walk with confidence in His plan. It provides peace in uncertainty, strength in trials, and clarity in confusion. Without His voice, we risk wandering aimlessly, much like a ship without a compass. Proverbs 3:5-6 captures this truth: "Trust in the Lord with all your heart and lean not on your own understanding; in all your ways submit to Him, and He will make your paths straight."

His voice is also a safeguard against the distractions and deceptions of the world. It helps us avoid false positives—situations or choices that appear good but ultimately lead us away from His purpose. Through His voice, we are reminded of our identity in Him and are anchored in His promises. When we are attuned to His Word, we can filter out the noise of fleeting ambitions, doubts, and worldly pressures, keeping our focus on the path He has set for us.

God's Voice vs. the Noise of the World

Every moment, the world bombards us with countless voices—those of society, culture, our thoughts, and even the enemy. These voices can be loud, persuasive, and distracting, but they lack the clarity and peace that come from God's Word. Recognizing God's voice becomes critical to distinguishing truth from lies.

Much like the sounds in nature—bird calls, the rustling of leaves, the hum of insects—each voice in our lives carries its own tone and purpose. Scientists have developed technology to identify these sounds, ensuring the protection of ecosystems. In a similar way, God calls us to recognize His voice for the preservation of our spiritual lives. Listening to Him helps us navigate the present and build a future aligned with His plan.

How do we differentiate God's voice from our own thoughts or the enemy's whispers? God's voice is marked by peace, confirmation, and alignment with His Word. As John 10:27 declares, "My sheep listen to my voice; I know them, and they follow me." The closer we walk with God, the easier it becomes to recognize His voice. Just as you instinctively recognize the voice of a loved one, familiarity with God grows through consistent time spent in prayer, worship, and Scripture.

Lessons from Technology: The Analogy of AI

Artificial intelligence offers an intriguing parallel for understanding how to hear God's voice. For example, convolutional neural networks (CNNs) are designed to identify patterns, whether in images or sounds, such as bird calls or species in a forest. These systems learn by analyzing vast amounts of data and are fine-tuned to detect what matters most.

In the same way, God has equipped us with spiritual "receptors" to recognize His voice. Just as AI requires precise training and calibration, we need to align our hearts with His truth. This happens through the consistent study of Scripture, prayer, and listening for His guidance. Where AI helps protect ecosystems, God's voice preserves our souls, guiding us toward His perfect will.

However, unlike artificial intelligence, which is limited by its programming, God's voice is infinite, personal, and perfectly tailored to each of us. His guidance is not a generic output but a direct call to our hearts, filled with love and purpose. While AI analyzes external data, God's voice speaks to our innermost being, addressing not just what we do but who we are.

The Power of Proximity

The closer we are to God, the easier it is to recognize His voice. Proximity builds familiarity, and familiarity builds trust. Just as a child learns to recognize a parent's voice amid a crowd, we learn to hear God's voice through a relationship. Spending time in His presence through prayer, worship, and meditating on His Word sharpens our spiritual ears.

Jesus illustrates this intimacy in John 15:5: "I am the vine; you are the branches. If you remain in me and I in you, you will bear much fruit; apart from me, you can do nothing." Remaining in Him means maintaining a constant connection, allowing His voice to guide and nourish us daily.

The Dangers of Misinterpreting Voices

Not every voice we hear comes from God, and this is where discernment becomes essential. False positives—voices that seem right but lead to spiritual dead ends—can deceive us into acting out of fear, pride, or misplaced priorities. For example, a career opportunity that promises success but compromises integrity might seem like a blessing but could pull us away from God's plan.

Jeremiah 17:9 warns, "The heart is deceitful above all things and beyond cure. Who can understand it?" Our emotions, while valid, can cloud our judgment if not anchored in God's truth. God's voice, however, is never misleading. It brings peace, aligns with His Word, and often requires faith but never contradicts His character.

CHAPTER 21:
THE VALUE OF GOD'S PRESENCE IN OUR LIVES

We often find ourselves striving—seeking meaning, purpose, and fulfillment in relationships, achievements, or possessions. Yet, without God at the center, these pursuits are like zeros lined up endlessly. No matter how many zeros we accumulate, their value remains unchanged unless a "1" is placed at the front. That "1" is Jesus Christ. He alone transforms the meaningless into the meaningful, the insignificant into the eternal.

To grasp this truth, consider this analogy: Suppose you possess everything the world deems valuable—wealth, power, relationships—but lack God. These things, like zeros, contribute no eternal significance. It is only when Jesus is placed at the forefront that your life gains infinite value. With Him, even the smallest effort, the humblest offering, or the quietest moment of faith becomes part of something immeasurably greater.

The Divine Mathematics of Humility

In the world's system, value is determined by wealth, power, status, or accomplishments. The more you accumulate, the higher your perceived worth. But God's economy operates on an entirely different principle. In His kingdom, greatness is not measured by climbing upward but by bowing downward.

Jesus Himself taught this when He said, *"Whoever wants to become great among you must be your servant, and whoever wants to be first must be your slave"* (Matthew 20:26–27). In this paradoxical truth, the lower we go in humility, the higher God exalts us. The zeros of humility, when surrendered to God, become the building blocks of eternal significance.

Consider the example of Jesus, who *"humbled Himself by becoming obedient to death—even death on a cross"* (Philippians 2:8). His humility, unmatched in history, set the ultimate example of how lowering oneself before God results in the highest exaltation. *"Therefore God exalted Him to the highest place and gave Him the name that is above every name"* (Philippians 2:9). This is the divine multiplication of humility at work.

The Practical Multiplication of Zeros

Humility in service: Every time you serve others selflessly, you add a zero. Jesus washed the feet of His disciples, a task reserved for servants, demonstrating that greatness comes through serving others. When we follow His example, our humility adds zeros to the value of our lives.

Humility in relationships: When we choose forgiveness over bitterness, kindness over retaliation, and love over pride, we add zeros. Humility in relationships reflects Christ's love and invites His presence into our lives.

Humility in acknowledging weakness: Admitting our limitations and dependence on God adds zeros because it shifts the focus from self-reliance to God-reliance. Paul declared, *"For when I am weak, then I am strong"* (2 Corinthians 12:10). Our weakness becomes an opportunity for God's strength to shine through.

Humility in obedience: Each time we surrender our will to God, we add a zero. Obedience often requires us to lay down our pride and trust His plan, even when it doesn't make sense. Jesus' obedience to the Father, even unto death, added eternal value to His mission of salvation.

The Paradox of Greatness in Humility

The world tells us to seek recognition, power, and self-promotion to achieve greatness. But Jesus flips this concept entirely. He taught that those who humble themselves will be exalted (Matthew 23:12).

The farther we bow before God, the greater the multiplication of zeros in His equation. Imagine someone who humbles themselves deeply, serving others with no expectation of reward or recognition. To the world, this person may appear insignificant, but in God's kingdom, they are like a string of zeros multiplied by Christ's "1." Their life becomes one of profound value, touching countless others and bringing glory to God.

Living with Christ as the "1"

We are, by ourselves, like a "0." A zero, no matter how many times you multiply or add it, remains of no value. Even the people we love the most—our spouse, friends, or family—are also "0" in this sense because they are human-like us and limited in their capacity to give us true and eternal value.

Now imagine this: to give value to zero, we need a "1." Only Jesus, with his infinite power, love, and grace, has the ability to be that "1." When we place Jesus at the forefront of our lives, He turns our "0" into a "10." This is the incredible transformation that happens when we fully accept Him into our hearts.

The beauty of this truth deepens as we humble ourselves. The more we humble ourselves, the more "zeros" we add to our spiritual journey. If we lower ourselves to the point of being completely down-to-earth, our humility stretches like a long line of zeros: 000000000000000000000000000000000000000000000000000000 . On their own, these zeros have no value, no matter how many we add. But when we place Jesus as the "1" at the front of this sequence, the result is astounding. Suddenly, we have a value so immense it cannot even be read easily — 10000000000000000000000000000000000000000000000000000000 .

This is the power of God's presence in our lives. It's not just about adding value; it's about transforming us into something meaningful and eternal. The zeros alone do not bring value; they gain their worth only when Christ stands at the front. If we attempt to add zeros through prideful effort or self-glorification, they lose their significance. True humility is not about adding zeros ourselves but allowing Christ to define and multiply our worth.

Humility is not thinking less of ourselves but thinking of ourselves less. It is recognizing that all our gifts, talents, and opportunities come from God and are meant to reflect His glory, not ours. When we live with this perspective, our lives become a powerful testimony of His grace.

Humility as an Eternal Investment

Every time we humble ourselves, we align with God's eternal purpose. Acts of humility are like planting seeds that will grow and bear fruit long after this life ends. Consider the following examples of eternal investments through humility:

1. **Service to Others**: Each act of selfless service creates ripples that extend into eternity. When we serve without expecting recognition, we embody Christ's example, and our actions become treasures in heaven. Jesus declared, *"The greatest among you will be your servant"* (Matthew 23:11).

2. **Surrender to God**: Each time we lay down our will and trust God's plan, we align with His eternal design. Surrender may

feel like a loss at the moment, but it is actually a gain, as God works through our humility to achieve His perfect purposes.

3. **Obedience in Small Things**: Humility teaches us that no act of obedience is too small to matter. Whether it's a kind word, a patient response, or a private prayer, these moments are treasures that contribute to God's glory and our eternal reward.

4. **Forgiveness and Love**: When we forgive others, even when it's undeserved, or love those who cannot repay us, we mirror God's unconditional grace. These acts of humility leave an eternal imprint, reflecting the depth of Christ's love.

Humility as a Reflection of Christ

Humility is more than a virtue; it is the essence of Christ's character. When Jesus said, *"Learn from me, for I am gentle and humble in heart, and you will find rest for your souls"* (Matthew 11:29), He invited us into a life that mirrors His own. Christ's humility was not a denial of His divinity but a testament to His love. Though He was equal with God, He chose to empty Himself, taking the form of a servant (Philippians 2:6–7). To live humbly is to reflect this same heart of servanthood. It means laying down our rights, pride, and self-centered desires to serve others and glorify God. Each act of humility is like a brushstroke on the canvas of our lives, shaping us more into the image of Jesus. As we grow in humility, we grow in Christlikeness, embodying His love, grace, and gentleness.

Jesus demonstrated humility in every aspect of His life. He associated with the lowly, washed the feet of His disciples, and bore the weight of humanity's sin on the cross. His life was a continual outpouring of love and service. When we live humbly, we participate in this divine example. Every time we set aside our desires to care for others, every moment we choose forgiveness over bitterness, and every time we serve without seeking recognition, we echo Christ's humility. These choices, though often unseen and uncelebrated on earth, are precious in God's sight.

In eternity, the true impact of our humility will be revealed. Picture this: standing before God, surrounded by the glory of heaven, and seeing how your humble choices—prayers whispered in secret, sacrifices made in silence, and kindness extended without expectation—have touched lives and brought glory to God. The unnoticed moments that seemed small in the world's eyes will be unveiled as treasures of eternal worth. The ripple effects of a humble heart will become evident: relationships restored, faith strengthened, and lives drawn closer to God. These moments will not be a reflection of our effort but a testimony to the greatness of Christ in us.

Humility transforms how we live when we embrace an eternal perspective. The world measures success by achievements, but humility teaches us that true greatness lies in serving God and others. When we shift our focus from temporary recognition to eternal significance, every act of humility becomes an investment in God's kingdom. Each time we choose humility over pride, we align ourselves with God's eternal purposes. Serving others, forgiving those who hurt us, and surrendering our plans to God may seem like losses at the moment, but they are eternal gains. Jesus said, *"Whoever exalts himself will be humbled, and whoever humbles himself will be exalted"* (Matthew 23:12).

The world often sees humility as weakness or insignificance, but in God's kingdom, humility is the foundation of strength and purpose. It is through humility that we truly encounter God's grace. As James 4:6 says, *"God opposes the proud but shows favor to the humble."* Humility opens the door for God's power to work through us, transforming our lives and the lives of those around us. Living humbly means recognizing that every good thing we have—our gifts, talents, and opportunities—comes from God. It is not about diminishing ourselves but about exalting Him. By surrendering our lives to His purposes, we allow His greatness to shine through us.

Humility leaves a lasting legacy that outlives us. Consider the countless humble servants of God who have quietly shaped the world through their faithfulness. Their names may never be celebrated in history books, but their impact echoes in eternity. When we live humbly, we build a legacy not of our own greatness but of God's grace. The zeros we add through humility are multiplied by Christ's presence, creating a life of immeasurable value.

Let us live with the assurance that every humble act matters to God. Whether it's a word of encouragement, an unseen sacrifice, or a choice to forgive, these moments are treasures stored in heaven. They are not forgotten or overlooked but cherished by the One who sees all. Humility, then, is not a loss but the greatest gain. It aligns us with God's eternal purposes, multiplies the impact of our lives, and glorifies the One who leads us. As we bow lower, Christ lifts us higher—not for our glory, but as vessels of His grace and glory. Let us embrace the humility of Christ, knowing that it is not only the path to true greatness but also the way to eternal joy and fulfillment in Him. Every choice to live humbly is a reflection of Jesus, a testimony to His love, and an offering that will shine forever in God's kingdom.

A Call to Humble Greatness

Humility is not weakness but strength under God's control. Each act of humility adds zeros to our lives, magnifying the eternal value that Christ brings. The question is not how many zeros we can add but whether we have placed Jesus at the forefront, allowing Him to define our worth.

So, bow lower. Serve others. Surrender your pride. Let the One who is "1" multiply the zeros of your humility into a life of immeasurable impact for His kingdom. In this divine economy, the more we humble ourselves, the greater the value we reflect on His glory.

False Positives in the Context of God's Presence

False positives in this context are those deceptive beliefs or actions that seem to hold value but ultimately pull us away from the true worth and presence of God. They appear to be paths to fulfillment or success but lack the eternal significance that comes only through placing Jesus at the forefront of our lives.

1. The Illusion of Self-Sufficiency

One of the most common false positives is the belief that we can derive lasting value and meaning through our own efforts, talents, or achievements. The world often glorifies self-made success, but this mindset disregards the truth that everything we have comes from God. Psalm 127:1 reminds us, "Unless the Lord builds the house, the builders labor in vain." Striving for greatness without anchoring ourselves in God leads to exhaustion and emptiness, no matter how much we accomplish.

2. The Allure of Wealth and Possessions

Wealth and material possessions can be mistaken for indicators of a meaningful life. The more we acquire, the more zeros we may feel we are adding to our lives. Yet, Jesus warns us in Luke 12:15, "Watch out! Be on your guard against all kinds of greed; life does not consist in an abundance of possessions." Without God as the "1,"

155

these zeros contribute no true value and leave us longing for something deeper.

3. The Pursuit of Worldly Recognition

Seeking approval, praise, or validation from others can create a false sense of purpose. We may think, "If I achieve this or if people admire me, I will feel complete." However, this pursuit often becomes a trap, as the world's standards are ever-changing and fickle. Galatians 1:10 challenges us to ask, "Am I now trying to win the approval of human beings or God? If I were still trying to please people, I would not be a servant of Christ."

4. The Deceptive Nature of Busyness

Filling our lives with endless activities and responsibilities may create the illusion of productivity and significance. However, busyness without purpose can distract us from God's presence. As Jesus told Martha in Luke 10:41-42, "You are worried and upset about many things, but few things are needed—or indeed only one. Mary has chosen what is better, and it will not be taken away from her." True value comes from sitting at Jesus' feet and aligning our actions with His will.

5. Misplaced Identity in Relationships

Another false positive is placing our identity and worth in human relationships rather than in God. While relationships are a gift from God, they cannot replace Him. Relying on others to define our value often leads to disappointment and insecurity. Only God's love is perfect and unchanging, as stated in Romans 8:38-39: "For I am convinced that neither death nor life...nor anything else in all creation, will be able to separate us from the love of God that is in Christ Jesus our Lord."

6. The Illusion of Control

The belief that we can control every aspect of our lives is a false positive that creates anxiety and fear. Proverbs 19:21 says, "Many are the plans in a person's heart, but it is the Lord's purpose that prevails." When we try to orchestrate our lives without surrendering to God's sovereignty, we end up overwhelmed and out of alignment with His perfect plan.

7. Spiritual Pride

Even in our walk with God, spiritual pride can become a false positive. We may begin to think that our acts of service, knowledge of Scripture, or visible piety make us more righteous. Yet, Isaiah 64:6 reminds us that "all our righteous acts are like filthy rags" without the grace of God. True humility comes from recognizing our dependence on Him and giving Him the glory.

How False Positives Deceive Us

These false positives often seem appealing because they align with our natural desires for security, recognition, and purpose. They exploit our fears and insecurities, promising immediate gratification or relief. However, they ultimately lead us away from the lasting peace and fulfillment that comes only through God's presence.

The zeros of achievements, possessions, or human approval can create an illusion of value, but without Jesus at the forefront, they remain empty. By identifying these false positives and re-centering our lives on Christ, we can avoid the deception and experience the transformative power of His presence.

Overcoming False Positives

To overcome false positives, we must intentionally place Jesus at the forefront of every aspect of our lives. This means seeking Him first in prayer, surrendering our plans to His will, and filtering every decision through His Word. As Matthew 6:33 reminds us, "But seek first His kingdom and His righteousness, and all these things will be given to you as well."

Recognizing false positives requires discernment, humility, and a constant awareness of God's presence. By trusting in Him and rejecting the fleeting promises of the world, we can live lives of true value and eternal significance. Only then will the zeros of our efforts and experiences gain their ultimate worth, multiplied by the One who gives them meaning.

CONCLUSION:

ANCHORING IN TRUTH THROUGH CHRIST

This book has taken you on a journey through the many ways false positives infiltrate our lives, particularly in the spiritual realm. These deceptive "almost-truths" often appear convincing, like a mirage shimmering in the desert or the interplay of stars and sunlight that I described earlier. Yet, without Jesus in our lives, discerning truth from falsehood becomes nearly impossible.

False positives don't simply trick our minds; they cloud our hearts and distort our purpose. They lure us into complacency, mislead us with promises of fulfillment, and, most dangerously, draw us away from the One who holds all truth. But when Jesus is in your boat, guiding you through life's stormy seas, you gain the clarity, strength, and wisdom to navigate these deceptions. His presence transforms confusion into understanding and illuminates the path to your true calling.

Jesus is not just a guide but the foundation of all truth. If our lives are not anchored in Him, we risk being swept away by fleeting emotions, worldly ambitions, or cultural pressures. Yet, when we allow Him to be our compass, His light exposes every false positive and aligns us with the purpose for which we were created. His voice, His Word, and His Spirit become the unshakable framework through which we filter every decision, thought, and desire.

Throughout this book, we've explored how technology, nature, and everyday experiences offer metaphors for understanding our spiritual journey. Whether it's recognizing His voice amid the noise, finding the right path through the complexities of life, or humbling ourselves to reflect His image, each chapter pointed to one ultimate truth: life only gains eternal value when Jesus is at the forefront. Like the string of zeros I explained, no matter how many we accumulate, their worth is meaningless unless the "1" of Christ stands before them.

This is not a call to perfection but a call to surrender. To place Jesus at the center of your life is to choose truth over deception, purpose over aimlessness, and eternity over the fleeting pleasures of this world. It is an invitation to walk humbly with God, embracing His refining process and trusting His plan, even when it contradicts your understanding.

An Eternal Perspective

As you close this book, consider the significance of eternity. Your life is not a random series of events but a masterpiece crafted by the Creator Himself. Each moment, each decision, each step in obedience adds to the eternal story He is weaving through you. False positives may offer temporary satisfaction, but they cannot compare to the lasting joy and fulfillment found in Christ.

God does not call us to a life free of trials but to a life anchored in truth. The storms will come, but when Jesus is in your boat, you will not be shaken. The world will tempt you with shortcuts, but His way—though it may seem longer—is always better. The noise will try to drown out His voice, but in stillness and surrender, you will hear His call, clear and unmistakable.

A Final Charge

As you continue your journey, let this truth guide you: life's greatest purpose is not found in accomplishments, possessions, or even relationships but in knowing and glorifying God. Seek Him first, and everything else will fall into place. Test every thought, emotion, and decision against His Word, for it is the ultimate filter that reveals what is true. Trust in His timing, for He is never late. Rest in His presence, for in Him, you will find peace beyond understanding.

False positives will always try to deceive, but with Jesus at the helm, you have everything you need to stand firm in truth. Let your life reflect His light, your actions His love, and your purpose His glory. You are His, and in Him, you are complete. Go forward in faith, knowing that the One who began a good work in you will carry it to completion until the day of Christ Jesus (Philippians 1:6).

This is your call—to live as a beacon of truth in a world of shadows, to discern the eternal amidst the temporary, and to embrace the fullness of life that only comes through Christ. With Him, your life is no longer a series of empty zeros but a masterpiece of infinite value, written by the hand of God Himself.